The Story of Liberty

Marvin McKenzie

Copyright @2016 Marvin McKenzie

All Scriptures are taken from the King James Bible.

Published in the United States of America

Thank you for purchasing this book. I trust it will prove to be helpful and a blessing to you.

Should you find this book is helpful to you or if you have questions you would like to ask me, feel free to contact me. My e-mail address is mck6858@gmail.com.

Introduction

It seems to me that there are three peoples in the history of the human race who have uniquely championed liberty. They are:

- **The Jews**
- **The British**
- **The Americans**

I believe the Jews possess their intense desire for liberty due to their spiritual heritage. God made man to be free. Satan robbed man from that liberty and the Jews are God's first step in the restoration of liberty. England, I believe, has roots in liberty because she was very early influenced by Christianity. Americans, in turn, are set on liberty because of our Christian roots inherited from England.

This book is an attempt to trace the steps of liberty through the Word of God. I use anecdotes primarily from the Revolutionary war as illustrations of principles of liberty found in God's Word. I am not a historian by any means. If some of the details in my anecdotes are flawed, it is not intentional. I do trust that my readers will forgive those flaws and head straight to the intent of the message.

Index

Chapter One

TRUE LIBERTY

Genesis 1:26-31

I cannot imagine that there is any living soul who does not long to be free. I believe it is bred into us – part of the divine likeness that, though corrupted through sin, is part of the original nature of our being. I find it to be curious that, in the history of mankind, there are two groups of people who have been the most focused on liberty:

- **The Jews**
- **The Christians**

In the history of Western Civilization, those people who have championed freedom are:

- **First the British**
- **Followed by Americans**

That is interesting because the Baptists in the British Isles (Wales in particular) have always insisted that theirs is an unbroken chain of Baptist doctrine tracing back to the Apostles of Jesus Christ.

That the British Isles has a unique link on liberty is historically undeniable. Almost from the beginning of their Monarchies, when King Alfred[1] in the 10th Century had parts of the Bible translated into the Old English and distributed among his citizens, the British have held to a higher form of government than any other people in Europe. In the height of the monarchies of Europe, England's monarchy stood alone – it is labeled "British Exceptionalism"[2] because their monarch has never been a totalitarian one. They were the envy of the people of Europe and they were the ire of the Monarch's of Europe because it was always understood that the British people, though having a Monarch, ruled themselves. As early as the

4

900's AD they had trials by jury rather judgments handed down by the King, an indication of their rule over one another.

The Magna Carta of AD 1225[3] was not so much the beginning of liberty in England as it was a document reinforcing what already existed in England. The people of England were free men. And although it was often challenged and never practiced perfectly it was always understood that the people of England had the right to rise up and replace their leaders if they did not keep their end of the contract with their citizens.

This is why, when the thirteen colonies fought for independence from England, they were within their rights as British citizens and not in violation against God's blessings. Thomas Jefferson said as much in the Declaration of Independence, "…Prudence, indeed, will dictate that Governments long established should not be changed for light and transient causes; and accordingly all experience hath shewn, that mankind are more disposed to suffer, while evils are sufferable, than to right themselves by abolishing the forms to which they are accustomed. But when a long train of abuses and usurpations, pursuing invariably the same Object evinces a design to reduce them under absolute Despotism, it is their right, it is their duty to throw off such Government and to provide new Guards for their future security…"

I want to begin at the only period of human history when I think an argument can be made that there was perfect liberty before Adam and Eve sinned in the Garden of Eden. I am sure there is someone who would challenge me, but I am convinced that man was created perfectly free.

I see three characteristics of this state of perfect liberty:

THEY HAD DOMINION OVER THE EARTH

(Though they did need to subdue it.)
Genesis 1:26, 28

Both the words subdue and dominion, have as a primary meaning, to tread under foot. God gave Adam and Eve – and their children – liberty to possess a piece of land:

- **To till it**
- **To inhabit it**
- **To work it and to make it to produce**

John Locke took from that man's inalienable right, he said, to "life, liberty and the pursuit of property." God gave Adam and Eve – and their children – liberty to govern the earth. In this case it was the

- **Fish**
- **Fowl**
- **Cattle**
- **Creeping things**

He has liberty to possess a piece of land, to till it, to enclose it and to put beasts of burden within it. John Locke argued that since the American Indians had never actually fenced a piece of property, it was technically not theirs. If you study much about the founding fathers of our country, you will learn that a good number of them were obsessed with possessing land and were skilled in the trade of surveying. They believed in the liberty to:

- **Mark out a piece of property**
- **Claim it as their own**
- **Put it to work**

Liberty, according to Locke, was the pursuit of property. You don't have a right to property; you have a right to earn property. God did not give us liberty to be lazy and receive without labor – not even before the fall. Adam and Eve were as free as any people have ever been, but they were free to gain through work; not free to get without working.

We live in a corrupt world and the truest of souls practice truth imperfectly. But the modern liberal concept that the wealthy own it to the poor to share their wealth with them is contrary to the "perfect law of liberty."

- **To give a person an opportunity to work is a noble thing**
- **To give a person the means to survive without working is to rob him of something more valuable than life – his dignity**

In a world of perfect liberty, they had dominion over the earth.

THEY HAD LIBERTY IN THEIR APPETITES

(Though there was a restriction.)
Vs 29-30, 2v16-17

I am going to mess up the:
- **Evolutionary**
- **Vegetarian**
- **Tree hugging**
- **Environmentalist**

right now. Not only did Adam and Eve have the liberty to fence in the animals of the earth, they had the liberty to eat them. The evolutionist has fed us a line so deeply that even the average Christian thinks that the first people only ate fruits and vegetables. I want to ask you some questions: Why would Adam and Eve want to capture a fowl, a fish, a cow or a creeping thing if they only ate fruits and vegetables? Do you honestly think that God was giving them permission to possess an aquarium in their living room? Is it really possible that when God told them to have dominion over the fowl of the air, all that He meant was they could train a parrot to say, "Polly wants a cracker"?

John Gill writes (in the 1700's) concerning Genesis 1:26,

"That is, to catch them, and eat them; though in the after grant of food to man, no mention as yet is made of any other meat than the herbs and fruits of the earth; yet what can this dominion over fish and fowl signify, unless it be a power to feed upon them?"

Gill understood, 100 years before Darwin came up with The Origin of the Species, that when God gave Adam and Eve liberty to have dominion over fowl, fish, cattle and creeping things – they were gonna eat them!

Taken together, verses 29-30 can be read to mean that
- **Every herb**
- **Every tree**
- **Every fruit**
- **Every beast of the earth**
- **Every fowl of the air**
- **Every thing that creepeth upon the earth**

has been given to eat. We don't read it that way because we have been so conditioned to think that men were supposed to only eat:
- **Fruits**
- **Nuts**
- **Vegetables**

In a world of perfect liberty, there was perfect freedom to eat whatever God had created.

But there was one restriction.
Genesis 2:17
But of the tree of the knowledge of good and evil, thou shalt not eat of it: for in the day that thou eatest thereof thou shalt surely die.

It is a perverted sense of liberty that thinks freedom means NO rules. It is impossible to live above the animals without rules.

I have a German Shorthaired Pointer.

- **She loves to run and hunt and chase rabbits and fetch quail**
- **She loves to explore and be free**

But if I leave her outside unattended too long, do you know what she does? She gets in her kennel. She knows in there she is safe and she is not going to get in trouble.

Put a little child in a room
- **With someone who is not paying any attention to the child; who gives that child absolute liberty to do anything, anywhere the child wants**
- **With someone who pays attention to the child, who lets the child know what he or she can and cannot do**

The child will gravitate to the person who cares enough to place some restrictions in his or her life because he or she knows that person cares about them.

Adam and Eve lived in a perfect world of perfect liberty, but even there they had a restriction.

THEY HAD LIBERTY IN THEIR FELLOWSHIP WITH GOD

(Though He was and is God.)
Genesis 2:18

Notice just three words with me:
"...Lord God said..."

- **The Lord is the Self Existing One**
- **God is the Supreme or Mighty Being**
- **Said means that Adam spoke to Him**

Genesis 3:8
And they heard the voice of the LORD God walking in the garden in the cool of the day: and Adam and his wife hid themselves from the presence of the LORD God amongst the trees of the garden.

Though by Genesis 3:8 Adam and Eve had already sinned and their fellowship with God was broken, the implication of the phrase, *"walking in the garden in the cool of the day"* tells us that this was something they were used to.

- **This was a regular occurrence**
- **This was a part of daily life for the person who was perfectly free**

They were free to fellowship with God. They were free:
- **To speak with Him**
- **To listen to Him**
- **To walk along side Him**

But they always knew that He was the Supreme One. He had issued a command,
Genesis 2:16
And the LORD God commanded the man, saying, Of every tree of the garden thou mayest freely eat:

And He had given a warning if they disobeyed that command,
Genesis 2:17
But of the tree of the knowledge of good and evil, thou shalt not eat of it: for in the day that thou eatest thereof thou shalt surely die.

The freest person in the world is the person who knows God and knows his rightful place before God.

It is true that, because of the corruption of sin, the best a man can have on earth today is an imperfect liberty. Liberty is something we fight for – something we know we ought to possess – something that is an inalienable right that forever slips our grasp.

Except, that is, when we know Jesus Christ.
2 Corinthians 3:17

Through a saving knowledge of Jesus Christ any man or woman can be perfectly free:

- **Free from the condemnation of hell**
- **Free from the bondage of sin**
- **Free from the burden of guilt**
- **Free from the fear of death**
- **Free from the corruption of the world**

[1]http://en.wikipedia.org/wiki/Old_English_Bible_translations
[2] http://oyc.yale.edu/history/hist-202/lecture-3
[3] http://en.wikipedia.org/wiki/Magna_Carta

Chapter Two

WHEN LIBERTY WAS LOST
Genesis 3:1-10

Though the great majority of people who moved from Europe to this continent in the 1600's did so fleeing religious oppression and hoping for the freedom to worship God according to the dictates of their own consciences, each of them came to this new land to charter a government authorized by England and each of them prided themselves in being English free men. The fact was, they were not so free as they imagined. Each colony except Rhode Island and Pennsylvania forced the inhabitants to worship God according to the dictates of their own charter and there was very much persecution of those dwelling in those colonies who worshiped some way other than the charter allowed. (Baptists were persecuted from Massachusetts all the way down to South Carolina. Baptists were never free men on this continent until after the signing of the Bill of Rights.) But the majority of the inhabitants of the colonies considered themselves English free men. And the English prided themselves on being free men.

You have to consider that those in the American colonies fought to be thought of on equal footing as their brothers and sisters in England. They were citizens of England, but they were like step children or half brothers and sisters. They were English free men, just on a lower scale. And they longed to be respected by England.

- **They loved England**
- **They were proud to be English**
- **They revered everything that was English**

But like a boy who reveres his father and would do anything to make him proud, only to discover there is nothing they can do to make his father proud, the English free men in America could, in the eyes of the national Englishman, never measure up to true British standards.

- **They loved their king**
- **They loved their Parliament**
- **They loved their system of government**

because, as they understood it, they always had the right to take any grievances they might have with their government directly to the Parliament (or to the King, depending upon the circumstances). Then came a series of taxes placed upon the American produced goods; taxes the Americans felt were unfairly charged upon them:

- **England was at war with France and it was costing them a fortune**
- **England had had to bring troops to America to fight off the Indians during the French and Indian war, and that had been no small expense**

– so, in England's mind, the Americans ought to pay for it.

Everything was probably OK at this point. The Americans were unhappy about the taxes and they sent diplomats to England to do exactly what they have always believed was their right to do, address their grievances and have them fairly considered. That isn't what happened. They were, in their opinions, snubbed as second-class citizens before the English Parliament. At this point they do what they have also believed was their right to do as English free men, they protested. The protest turned ugly and shots were fired – people died. So they took the next step of an English free man – they raised a militia.

It was at this point the lights began to turn on and the thought came to their minds, "Our liberty has been lost." Right about now, March 23, 1775, Patrick Henry stood and delivered his famous "Give me liberty or give me death speech, the last part of which said,

"They tell us, sir, that we are weak; unable to cope with so formidable an adversary. But when shall we be stronger? Will it be the next week, or the next year? Will it be when we are totally disarmed, and when a British guard shall be stationed in every house? Shall we gather strength by irresolution and inaction? Shall we acquire the means of effectual resistance, by lying supinely on our backs, and hugging the delusive phantom of hope, until our enemies shall have bound us hand and foot? Sir, we are not weak if we make a proper use of those means which the God of nature hath placed in our power. Three millions of people, armed in the holy cause of liberty, and in such a country as that which we possess, are invincible by any force which our enemy can send against us. Besides, sir, we shall not fight our battles alone. There is a just God who presides over the destinies of nations; and who will raise up friends to fight our battles for us. The battle, sir, is not to the strong alone; it is to the vigilant, the active, the brave. Besides, sir, we have no election. If we were base enough to desire it, it is now too late to retire from the contest. There is no retreat but in submission and slavery! Our chains are forged! Their clanking may be heard on the plains of Boston! The war is inevitable and let it come! I repeat it, sir, let it come.

It is in vain, sir, to extenuate the matter. Gentlemen may cry, Peace, Peace but there is no peace. The war is actually begun! The next gale that sweeps from the north will bring to our ears the clash of resounding arms! Our brethren are already in the field! Why stand we here idle? What is it that gentlemen wish? What would they have? Is life so dear, or peace so sweet, as to be purchased at the price of chains and slavery? Forbid it, Almighty God! I know not what course others may take; but as for me, give me liberty or give me death!"[1]

Adam and Eve were perfectly free in the Garden of Eden but their liberty was lost. Let me give you several observations from the passage where Adam and Eve lost their liberty.

THEIR LIBERTY WAS LOST WHEN THEY DISOBEYED GOD

Genesis 2:16-17
And the LORD God commanded the man, saying, Of every tree of the garden thou mayest freely eat:
But of the tree of the knowledge of good and evil, thou shalt not eat of it: for in the day that thou eatest thereof thou shalt surely die.

Adam and Eve were perfectly free inside the Garden. True, the garden would have had perimeters. I do not know how large the Garden of Eden was. Nobody does. I read a short piece from Ken Ham of **Answers in Genesis** where he says that nobody really knows even where the Garden of Eden was. The earth was so different before the Flood that it is impossible to say. If we don't know where it was, we surely don't know how big it was.
- **It could have been huge**
- **It could have covered half the earth**
(I don't know that. I am simply exaggerating to make a point.) The point is that no matter how large the Garden of Eden was,

there was an end to the Garden; a border, which, once crossed, placed them outside of paradise.

Then there was this one limitation God gave them – a command – one thing they could not eat. They were absolutely free so long as they stayed inside the Garden and so long as they did not eat that one fruit. But they disobeyed God and found themselves banned from the Garden of Eden. A person could argue that now they were free:

- **They knew the difference between good and evil**
- **They ate the one thing they couldn't eat**
- **They were now outside of God's restrictions**

They were absolutely free of God's rule, and they were miserable. They were their own masters, and they hated it

I see people in bondage all around me:

- **Bondage to sin**
- **Bondage to fears**
- **Bondage to emotions**
- **Bondage to guilt**

And in every case the thing that binds them is their refusal to obey God.

THEIR LIBERTY WAS LOST AS THE RESULT OF AN ENEMY

Genesis 3:1-5

Now the serpent was more subtil than any beast of the field which the LORD God had made. And he said unto the woman, Yea, hath God said, Ye shall not eat of every tree of the garden?

And the woman said unto the serpent, We may eat of the fruit of the trees of the garden:

But of the fruit of the tree which is in the midst of the garden, God hath said, Ye shall not eat of it, neither shall ye touch it, lest ye die.

And the serpent said unto the woman, Ye shall not surely die:

For God doth know that in the day ye eat thereof, then your eyes shall be opened, and ye shall be as gods, knowing good and evil.

There are a lot of unexplained situations right here, aren't there?

- **How did the serpent speak?**
- **In what ways was it more subtle than other beasts (did they talk too?)**
- **Where was Adam when this whole conversation was going on?**
- **Why did he eat the fruit knowing it was wrong?**

There is one thing about the passage that strike me more than any other –the serpent, who is later revealed as the Devil[2] was an enemy to their liberty.

Here's your takeaway:

- **Anyone**
- **Anything**
- **Anyplace**

that tempts you to pull away from God is not your friend – he is an enemy.

- **He may say nice things**
- **He may appear to be on your side**
- **He may give you what you think are reasonable things to think about**

But if he, or it, tends to draw you away from God, count he or it an enemy! You can't afford to be kind to an enemy.

- **You don't have to hate him**
- **You don't have to hold a grudge against him**
- **You don't have to think evil things about him**

but you can't ever trust an enemy.

My wife likes to turn the car radio onto a station that plays Christmas music of all sorts. One of the songs is about Snoopy and the Bloody Red Baron. It's Christmas Eve when they meet in the skies. The Red Baron gets the better on Snoopy and he's going down for sure. But for whatever reason, maybe it was the Christmas bells ringing below; the Red Baron chooses not to shoot Snoopy down. He forces him to land behind enemy lines where he brings Snoopy a drink and they toast to Christmas. Snoopy then flies away, knowing the two would meet in the air another day – the next time one of the two would die. Whatever or whomever tries to pull you away from the close and personal walk with God is an enemy.

- **Count him as such**
- **Treat him as such**

THEIR LIBERTY WAS LOST AS A RESULT OF THEIR OWN ACTIONS

Genesis 3:6
And when the woman saw that the tree was good for food, and that it was pleasant to the eyes, and a tree to be desired to make one wise, she took of the fruit thereof, and did eat, and gave also unto her husband with her; and he did eat.

If you are familiar with the passage you know that there is a whole lot of blaming that goes on pretty soon.

- **Adam blames Eve**
- **Eve blames the serpent**
- **The serpent just crawls on the ground**

But the fact of the matter is that:

- **Eve listened to the serpent's temptations**
- **Eve looked at the fruit and decided to eat it**
- **Adam took the fruit from Eve and chose to eat it too**

When my oldest son was very young, he got into trouble and I gave him a spanking for it. Afterward he was pretty upset. He told me he hated the devil for making him do that. My answer was that the devil did not make him do anything. He got in trouble all on his own. The Devil will tempt us to disobey God, but he can't make us – especially if we are Christians. When we sin, we do that of our own choosing.

THE CONSEQUENCES OF LOST LIBERTY WAS GREATER THAN THEY WANTED TO PAY

Genesis 3:14-19

And the LORD God said unto the serpent, Because thou hast done this, thou art cursed above all cattle, and above every beast of the field; upon thy belly shalt thou go, and dust shalt thou eat all the days of thy life:

And I will put enmity between thee and the woman, and between thy seed and her seed; it shall bruise thy head, and thou shalt bruise his heel.

Unto the woman he said, I will greatly multiply thy sorrow and thy conception; in sorrow thou shalt bring forth children; and thy desire shall be to thy husband, and he shall rule over thee.

And unto Adam he said, Because thou hast hearkened unto the voice of thy wife, and hast eaten of the tree, of which I commanded thee, saying, Thou shalt not eat of it: cursed is the ground for thy sake; in sorrow shalt thou eat of it all the days of thy life;

Thorns also and thistles shall it bring forth to thee; and thou shalt eat the herb of the field;

In the sweat of thy face shalt thou eat bread, till thou return unto the ground; for out of it wast thou taken: for dust thou art, and unto dust shalt thou return.

Genesis 3:22-24

And the LORD God said, Behold, the man is become as one of us, to know good and evil: and now, lest he put forth his hand, and take also of the tree of life, and eat, and live for ever:

Therefore the LORD God sent him forth from the garden of Eden, to till the ground from whence he was taken.

So he drove out the man; and he placed at the east of the garden of Eden Cherubims, and a flaming sword which turned every way, to keep the way of the tree of life.

The unhappiest people I know are those who are out of fellowship with God. Whether they are:

- **Unsaved and living without hope of eternal life**
- **Saved and living in opposition to the revealed will of God**

No one is happy without the liberty found in Jesus Christ.

LIBERTY IS REGAINED IN THE GRACIOUS PROMISE OF GOD

Genesis 3:15
And I will put enmity between thee and the woman, and between thy seed and her seed; it shall bruise thy head, and thou shalt bruise his heel.

This is one of the greatest verses in the Bible, but maybe one of the least esteemed. It is the very first gospel promise and it was preached by none other than God. Adam and Eve had lost their liberty, but they were not left without hope. God's promise was that one day there would come One who would destroy their enemy and restore their liberty. We know that One to be Jesus Christ.

John 8:36
If the Son therefore shall make you free, ye shall be free indeed.

Conclusion

The founders of our country realized they had lost their liberty, but they too were not without hope. Liberty was worth having, even if the price to gain it was a high one. Liberty of the soul too is worth having. It is worth fighting for. It is worth sacrificing self so that I and my children may be free in Jesus Christ.

[1]http://www.history.org/almanack/life/politics/giveme.cfm
[2] Revelation 20:2
And he laid hold on the dragon, that old serpent, which is the Devil, and Satan, and bound him a thousand years,

Chapter Three

FREEDOM ISN'T FREE
Exodus 15:21-22

We celebrate our independence as a country every year on July Fourth. It is appropriate that we do so and it is the date our founding fathers acknowledged as the beginning of their own liberty. But the fact is that, though they had declared themselves free, they still had to earn it. The hard work for liberty was still ahead of them. The surrender of the British, signaling independence, did not happen until October 19, 1781. Even the surrender of England did not give these free men relief from hard work. At the time of the surrender of England, the United States was operating under a document called The Articles of Confederation. Some people wish we still were.

The Articles of Confederation provided that each states was like it's own independent nation, voluntarily cooperating with, for all practical purposes, an impotent federal government. Men like Patrick Henry and Sam Adams felt like anything more would be a worse government than the one they had just fought to be free from. When Patrick Henry heard of the convention to propose a Constitution of the United States, his exact words were, "I smell a rat." I am not a politician and can't pretend to understand these things much, but I tend to side with men like:

- **James Madison**
- **John Adams**
- **George Washington**

on this one.[1]

The country was very young. The cost of the war had been enormous, and, because of the voluntary nature of the Confederation, there was no way for the Federal Government to get the money necessary to pay the debts of the War for Independence. People like James Madison, Alexander Hamilton and John Jay worked on the Federalist Papers, a series of articles meant to convince the public of the need of a centralized government. Men like Patrick Henry and Richard Henry Lee rebutted with the Anti-Federalist Papers. The constitutional convention met in Philadelphia in May of 1787, very nearly six years after the Surrender at Yorktown. Through the very hot summer months of 1787 the delegates labored in a hot, sealed room, hammering out the document that has governed our nation for just over 227 years. When the work was done, the citizens of Philadelphia were anxious to learn what had happened. A woman named Mrs. Powel asked Benjamin Franklin, "Well, Doctor, what have we got, a republic or a monarchy?" With no hesitation whatsoever, Franklin responded, "A republic, if you can keep it."[2] Franklin understood the very difficult truth about freedom; freedom isn't free.

That's a lesson Israel was about to learn in the wilderness between Egypt and their Promised Land.

- **They had cried to God for freedom when they were slaves in Egypt**
- **Before too long they will be crying out, wishing they could go back to Egypt**

Freedom isn't free. One of the key principles of Baptist believers over two thousand years of history has been the doctrine of "Individual Soul Liberty." That became a principle doctrine among our nations founding fathers. Through a process the founders of our country, almost all of them culturally convinced that our new country had to select a church denomination as our official government church, and then tax every American to support its pastors and build its buildings. Gave in to the idea that the inalienable right to life, liberty and the pursuit of happiness, necessitated them to worship God according to the dictate of one's own conscience. These ideas were planted into the minds of

- **Patrick Henry**
- **James Madison**
- **Thomas Jefferson**

among others, by the Baptists.

Liberty means different things to different people, but one of the things it most certainly means to Americans is that we each have the right – the liberty – to worship God, or not to worship Him at all, according to the dictates of our own conscience. But individual soul liberty, like any other type of liberty, never comes without a price.

I want to give you three observations then from the Jews, fresh out as free men and women.

LIBERTY IS NOT WITHOUT LOSS (Sacrifice)
Exodus 15:21-22

Israel was free, but they were between two to seven million people in a wilderness:

- **Without food**
- **Without water**
- **Without means to get these things**

They were completely dependent upon the God they had cried out to for deliverance from Egypt.

One of the most challenging things about liberty is that, while there is great potential for gain, there is also an initial loss that comes. The slaves, freed by Abraham Lincoln's emancipation proclamation learned that.

- **They were free men – no longer bound to their wealthy plantation masters**
- **They were also unemployed men – no longer able to feed themselves and their families**

Men like Thomas Jefferson and George Washington knew that slavery was immoral and had to be abolished but they also knew that it was impractical to just let them all go. They didn't have the answers as to how to transition the economy of the agricultural south and the needs of the huge numbers of blacks, if they were immediately set free, but they did understand that to let them all free on a moment's notice would mean hardship not only to the plantation owners, but to the freed slaves as well.

Israel was free. And three days – just three days after being free once and for all, they were without water. After thirty days they were without food and starving – crying for the luxuries of Egypt.
Exodus 16:2-3 KJV
And the whole congregation of the children of Israel murmured against Moses and Aaron in the wilderness:
And the children of Israel said unto them, Would to God we had died by the hand of the LORD in the land of Egypt, when we sat by the flesh pots, and when we did eat bread to the full; for ye have brought us forth into this wilderness, to kill this whole assembly with hunger.

I got saved in April of 1977. I was baptized December 16, 1979. With my baptism I gained some wonderful things:

- **A family of believers that loved me and were a joy to be around**[3]
- **A best friend in Mike Riggs, who to this day is the most important human being I know with the exception of my wife**
- **A pastor who knew the Bible and preached it in ways that thrilled me**

But I also lost some things:

- **I lost some friends I had grown up with around the rodeo**
- **I lost some respect among some of the men that I worked with**
- **I lost the very close relationship I had with my mom**
- **I lost my brothers and sisters, all of whom rejected my faith**

- **I lost my weekends to do with as I pleased**
- **I lost Wednesday nights to church services**
- **I lost the tithe of my income[4]**
- **I lost a lifestyle I thought was without boundaries**

- **I lost habits I thought I enjoyed at the time**
- **I lost a language I had become used to**

The signers of the Declaration of Independence were, for the most part, successful, well paid men with property, businesses and status in their communities. The last line of the Declaration reads, "And for the support of this Declaration, with a firm reliance on the protection of divine Providence, we mutually pledge to each other our Lives, our Fortunes and our sacred Honor." They knew that the liberty they sought would cost them.

LIBERTY IS NOT LAZINESS (Work)

Numbers 13:30-33 KJV

And Caleb stilled the people before Moses, and said, Let us go up at once, and possess it; for we are well able to overcome it.

But the men that went up with him said, We be not able to go up against the people; for they are stronger than we.

And they brought up an evil report of the land which they had searched unto the children of Israel, saying, The land, through which we have gone to search it, is a land that eateth up the inhabitants thereof; and all the people that we saw in it are men of a great stature.

And there we saw the giants, the sons of Anak, which come of the giants: and we were in our own sight as grasshoppers, and so we were in their sight.

Numbers 14:1-4 KJV
And all the congregation lifted up their voice, and cried; and the people wept that night.
And all the children of Israel murmured against Moses and against Aaron: and the whole congregation said unto them, Would God that we had died in the land of Egypt! or would God we had died in this wilderness!
And wherefore hath the LORD brought us unto this land, to fall by the sword, that our wives and our children should be a prey? were it not better for us to return into Egypt?
And they said one to another, Let us make a captain, and let us return into Egypt.

Very early on Israel learned that their liberty was going to amount to some work.

And their first taste of it, repulsed them. They had done hard labor before, but this was a different kind of work.

- **They would have to possess the Promised Land**
- **It wasn't going to be given to them without some blood sweat and tears**

There was other work they had to do as well:

- **Construct a Tabernacle**
- **Organize a government**
- **Create a system of worship**

The Bible says 2 Thessalonians 3:10 KJV
For even when we were with you, this we commanded you, that if any would not work, neither should he eat.

That's true physically.

I just read this week about a speech Davie Crockett[5] gave while serving as a Representative in Congress. The widow of a congressman was in need and the house was considering a vote to give her a sum of money for the government to help her in her need. Just prior to the vote Davie Crockett stepped up to the platform and spoke. He told the Congressmen that the Constitution did not give them authority to give away the money that the citizens of the country had paid in to the government. He said that, while he would have to vote against giving her the money out of the nation's treasury, he was willing to give her a week of his salary and pointed out that if every congressman did the same it would amount to more than they were voting to give her anyway. The congressmen did not pass the vote. Someone later asked Crockett why he said what he said. He told them that one of his constituents; a man who had voted for him in a previous election, had rebuked him kindly and said he would not vote for him ever again. When Crockett asked why, the man remarked about a previous bill concerning the Constitution that the Congress had unanimously passed, (including Crockett) to give aide to a community that had been destroyed by fire. This man taught him that the Constitution, in order to be of any value at all, must be held sacred and that it in no way gave Congress authority to give away the money in its coffers for such benevolence. He explained the Constitution's parameters and sacredness to Crockett so clearly that Crockett said, "Before I vote to tamper with the Constitution ever again, I will take a bullet."

Knowing Crockett's end, I think he meant it.

Franklin Delano Roosevelt, I think, was the first one to make it a responsibility of our government to give handouts to the needy. You might think it has made us a kinder more humane people but it has resulted in two tragic things:

- **It has led to several generations of Americans now who believe government owes them a living**
- **It has put us in debt to the point it will very likely ruin our nation**

It's also true spiritually.

No one really grows spiritually who doesn't work at growing in grace and in the knowledge of our Lord and Saviour Jesus Christ. We have come to the place where we think we are to occupy ourselves with the business of living and we pay the pastor to teach us the Bible so we don't have to learn it ourselves.

The modern Christian concept is:
- **Preachers are called to study the Bible and tell us what it says**
- **Preachers are called to go into the highways and compel people to come into church**
- **Preachers are called to be there to give me comfort whenever I am down**

Preachers are called to do those things and we pay them good money to get it done. But the fact is:
- **What a preacher does from the pulpit will have almost no value if the congregation isn't faithfully studying the Bible for themselves**
- **Preachers are to be witnesses, but they will never be as effective at personal witnessing as you will be with your neighbors, family and co-workers**
- **Preachers can't bring comfort to anyone who hasn't already received comfort from the Holy Spirit**

You have the freedom to worship God according to the dictates of your own conscience, but if you haven't studied the Word of God,
- **You are a slave to the will of the flesh**
- **You are a slave to the ideas of your pastor**

Even if your pastor is right, you don't want to depend upon him spiritually.
- **He should aide you**
- **He should not carry you**

LIBERTY IS NOT LICENSE (Irresponsibility)

Numbers 25:1-8 KJV

And Israel abode in Shittim, and the people began to commit whoredom with the daughters of Moab.

And they called the people unto the sacrifices of their gods: and the people did eat, and bowed down to their gods.

And Israel joined himself unto Baal-peor: and the anger of the LORD was kindled against Israel.

And the LORD said unto Moses, Take all the heads of the people, and hang them up before the LORD against the sun, that the fierce anger of the LORD may be turned away from Israel.

And Moses said unto the judges of Israel, Slay ye every one his men that were joined unto Baalpeor.

And, behold, one of the children of Israel came and brought unto his brethren a Midianitish woman in the sight of Moses, and in the sight of all the congregation of the children of Israel, who were weeping before the door of the tabernacle of the congregation.

And when Phinehas, the son of Eleazar, the son of Aaron the priest, saw it, he rose up from among the congregation, and took a javelin in his hand;

And he went after the man of Israel into the tent, and thrust both of them through, the man of Israel, and the woman through her belly. So the plague was stayed from the children of Israel.

This is a gruesome passage without question. I am glad we don't do things like this today. But it does teach the lesson that being free does not make us free to live in wanton sin.

- **A person does not have to worship God the same way I do**
- **A person does not have to believe the same doctrines I do**
- **A person doesn't even have to read the same Scriptures I do**

We are free to follow our own consciences in those matters. But no person has the right to:

- **Kill a baby because it inconveniences their lifestyle or**
- **Marry a person of the same sex because that is what their flesh lusts**
- **Behead a person because their religion teaches he or she is an infidel**

Freedom is not free.

- **It always comes at a price**
- **It offers opportunity for personal work, but it in no way releases us from work**
- **It always comes with boundaries over which no free man can ever cross**

[1] Jefferson was in France at the time.

[2] http://www.ourrepubliconline.com/Author/21, accessed 1-24-15

[3] I had gained my freedom from the penalty of sin when I got saved.

[4] I speak concerning my weekends and tithe as a man would speak. I never lost anything by giving them to God.

[5] http://fee.org/library/detail/not-your-to-give-2, accessed 1-24-15 Part of the constituent's argument was, "The power of collecting and disbursing money at pleasure is the most dangerous power that can be entrusted to man, particularly under our system of collecting revenue by a tariff, which reaches every man in the country, no matter how poor he may be, and the poorer he is the more he pays in proportion to his means….

…it is a precedent fraught with danger to the country, for when Congress once begins to stretch its power beyond the limits of the Constitution, there is no limit to it, and no security for the people."

Chapter Four

FREEDOM FIGHTERS

Joshua 13:1 KJV

Now Joshua was old and stricken in years; and the LORD said unto him, Thou art old and stricken in years, and there remaineth yet very much land to be possessed.

While our forefathers, from the beginning, sent ambassadors to others countries:

- **Thomas Jefferson**
- **John Adams**
- **Benjamin Franklin**

each served as early American ambassadors. But in every case, their work was to bolster trade with those nations. And in order to grow our economy through free trade with those countries, our official position in issues of war was one of isolationism. We just did not get involved. Our policy was to stay out of our friends' fights, choosing only to take up arms when our own interests were being threatened.

That was the case with the war of 1812. America's policy concerning the Napoleonic wars was one of strict isolationism.

- **We conducted trade with England**
- **We also conducted trade with France**

As far as our founding fathers were concerned, this war was their war and not our own. We wanted to do business with them both. Until England attempted to hinder our trade with France.

- **British ships of war would capture an American merchant ship and force the sailors to serve in the Royal Navy**
- **Britain sent ships to block access to and from American ports so we cold not send or receive goods from France**

America's position during the War of 1812 was that we were at war with England. England's position was that America was merely one theatre of operation in their war with France.

The United States was involved in another war between the American Revolution and the War of 1812. Between 1801 and 1805 our forefathers fought the First Barbary Coast War against the Muslim states of Tripoli, Algiers and Tunis. The tension between the U.S. and the Barbary Coast states had existed since the end of the Revolutionary War. President Washington sent John Adams and Thomas Jefferson as the principle players attempting to negotiate peaceful relationships. When the pirates captured a U.S. merchant ship and held its sailors captive for ransom, our representative asked why they had taken these prisoners unprovoked. The Muslims answered:

> "It was written in their Koran, that all nations which had not acknowledged the Prophet were sinners, whom it was the right and duty of the faithful to plunder and enslave; and that every mussulman who was slain in this warfare was sure to go to paradise."[1]

John Adams recommended that America pay the ransom. I understand that we paid yearly tributes to these pirate states throughout the presidencies of Washington and Adams. Thomas Jefferson was of the opinion that paying them a ransom would encourage them to further acts of violence and urged that we raise a navy at once and go to war. Jefferson, who was at the time our ambassador to France, wrote to Adams saying,

> "I acknowledge [sic] I very early thought it would
> be best to effect a peace thro' the medium of war."
> Paying tribute will merely invite more demands,
> and even if a coalition proves workable, the only

solution is a strong navy that can reach the pirates, Jefferson argued in an August 18, 1786, letter to James Monroe: "The states must see the rod; perhaps it must be felt by some one of them. . . . Every national citizen must wish to see an effective instrument of coercion and should fear to see it on any other element than the water. A naval force can never endanger our liberties, nor occasion bloodshed; a land force would do both." "From what I learn from the temper of my countrymen and their tenaciousness of their money," Jefferson added in a December 26, 1786, letter to the president of Yale College, Ezra Stiles, "it will be more easy to raise ships and men to fight these pirates into reason, than money to bribe them."[2]

To summarize Jefferson's recommendation, he said that we had only two options concerning the Muslims:
* **Buy them off**
* **Fight them**
And he said it would be, in the long run, far less expensive to fight them than to bribe them.

Other than issues like that, our forefathers' choice was to keep to themselves and seek to advance the cause of the United States. This position of strict isolationism was, as far as I understand, the doctrine of American international politics through to at least the end of WWI.

America did not enter WWI until Germany picked a fight with us. With the end of WWI, we entered into a period of international policy called "limited internationalism."
- **We were aware of issues of other nations**

- **We might side with one nation or another, offering supplies and other necessities for the war**

but we tried to stay out of the battle.

WWII changed all of that. We entered WWII under the doctrine of "limited internationalism". In other words, we sought to help England against German by supplying them with the things they needed to successfully fight the Germans, but we tried to stay out of the battle ourselves. We only entered the contest when Germany once again made it our fight.

The end of WWII saw a dramatic shift in American policy concerning international relations.

- **The United Nations was formed, and the US joined it**
- **The United States intervened in the Middle East, helping to create an official Jewish State**
- **Though Russia had been an ally during WWII, the outcome of that war was that the US and communist Russia became competing superpowers**

Under President Truman a new international doctrine developed called "Containment/Counterforce". The concept was this; without actually going to war with Communist Russia, we would press against their boundaries in an effort to prevent communism from spreading. It was at this point that America came to this understanding, Freedom is worth sharing. They rightly saw communism as a threat to personal liberty.

- **Communism denies the individual the right to freely earn**
- **Communism denounces the individual's right to possess property**
- **Communism deprives the individual's right to worship God according to the dictates of his own conscience**

The differences between communism and capitalism are not merely differences of opinion about how wealth is shared – they are fundamental differences about those things our forefathers believed to be inalienable rights. With the rise of communism, Americans realized that liberty/freedom must not only be maintained, it must be expanded.

*** To stop growing freedom will lead to**
*** Taking freedom for granted**
*** Then freedom will begin to wither and die**

Satan is the enemy of liberty. If we do not fight for freedom, we will eventually lose it.

So the children of Israel had entered the Promised Land and possessed it.
Joshua 11:23 KJV
So Joshua took the whole land, according to all that the LORD said unto Moses; and Joshua gave it for an inheritance unto Israel according to their divisions by their tribes. And the land rested from war.

The land was divided among the tribes and the two and half tribes who had received their portion on the other side of the Jordan River were allowed to return home. Yet the Lord said to them,
Joshua 13:1 KJV
…. there remaineth yet very much land to be possessed.

I want to warn you that there is no such thing as a rest in the battle for freedom of conscience; the liberty to worship God according to the dictates of your own conscience.
- **The moment you rest in your liberty to worship God**
- **You will begin to take that liberty for granted**
- **You will begin to walk away, to lose that liberty to worship God according to the dictates of your own conscience**

I want to suggest to you three areas in your life where you must never stop fighting for spiritual freedom:

IN THE AREA OF PERSONAL GROWTH

Joshua 14:6-12 KJV

Then the children of Judah came unto Joshua in Gilgal: and Caleb the son of Jephunneh the Kenezite said unto him, Thou knowest the thing that the LORD said unto Moses the man of God concerning me and thee in Kadesh-barnea.

Forty years old was I when Moses the servant of the LORD sent me from Kadesh-barnea to espy out the land; and I brought him word again as it was in mine heart.

Nevertheless my brethren that went up with me made the heart of the people melt: but I wholly followed the LORD my God.

And Moses sware on that day, saying, Surely the land whereon thy feet have trodden shall be thine inheritance, and thy children's for ever, because thou hast wholly followed the LORD my God.

And now, behold, the LORD hath kept me alive, as he said, these forty and five years, even since the LORD spake this word unto Moses, while the children of Israel wandered in the wilderness: and now, lo, I am this day fourscore and five years old.

As yet I am as strong this day as I was in the day that Moses sent me: as my strength was then, even so is my strength now, for war, both to go out, and to come in.

Now therefore give me this mountain, whereof the LORD spake in that day; for thou heardest in that day how the Anakims were there, and that the cities were great and fenced: if so be the LORD will be with me, then I shall be able to drive them out, as the LORD said.

Caleb is, to me, one of the most inspiring people in the Bible. He was one of the twelve spies who Moses had sent into the Promised Land and Kadesh Barnea more than forty years previous and He was one of only two of those spies[3] who at that time urged the people of Israel to trust God and take the land. Caleb and Joshua were the only two men over the age of twenty when Kadesh Barnea occurred, to live through the forty years in the wilderness. Even Moses and Aaron had died without seeing the Promised Land.

Caleb plays a relatively insignificant role through the forty years in the wilderness and at least not a public role during the conquest of the Promised Land. But here he steps back out into the limelight of faith. Moses had made a promise to him forty-five years earlier. He had seen a piece of property he liked and, though he is 85 years old – he wants permission from Joshua to go take it.

If Caleb, at 85, could storm a mountain, there is no reason you and I should ever stop pressing ourselves on for spiritual growth. Except that, after a while, that the battles we need to fight, get harder.

I've been a Christian now since 1977. And though I still have plenty of spiritual property I need to possess, it is more difficult now than it was for me thirty years ago – I think for at least two reasons:
A. A lot of people think I have possessed enough land
Some would say that for me to take the steps that I need to take now would be downright fanatical.

You know some of those sorts of Christians, don't you? They think a little bit of religion is fine – just don't let it change your life. They say things like "Don't become so heavenly minded you are no earthly good."

These sorts of people like to throw around the word, "legalism." If you want to attend church services now and then, well they would say, "More power to you!" But if you ever got to the place where you believed you should be in church unless providentially hindered, they would call you a legalist.

The fact is that one of the most difficult things I face about growing spiritually now is that, so many people think I have gone too far as it is!

Israel had the land, didn't they? Caleb's tribe has already gotten their lot hadn't they? Why does Caleb need to take any more? He's a fanatic!

May I say that you ought to be a spiritual fanatic too?

B. There are fewer who will fight alongside me
Think about Israel back in Caleb's day.
- **The two and half tribes have their possession on the other side of the Jordan – they want to go home**
- **The other nine and half tribes have already gotten their lots. They want to begin tilling their ground**

There just aren't very many people left who want to take on that extra bit on Caleb's behalf.

The longer I am a Christian the fewer it seems who are willing to take on spiritual battles any more. For one thing, there are fewer of them who see these mountains that are left to take as necessary. After 38 years
- **I am fairly moral**
- **I have a pretty decent grasp of the Bible**
- **My wife, my kids, and I are doing pretty well**
- **I have a decent ministry**
- **I am respected among my pastoral peers (for the most part)**

And then there are, in my opinion unfortunately, a lot of those who used to strive for spiritual growth with me, who have turned around.
- **They don't want to be called legalists any more**
- **They don't want to be thought of as fanatics any more**
- **They don't want to be heavenly minded any more**

- **A lot of pastors who used to believe like I do about the King James Version of the Bible have backed off now**
- **A lot of the pastors who used to preach Baptist distinctives have compromised the Baptist name now**
- **A lot of Christians who used to live with high standards have dropped those standards now**

And it makes the battle to press on more challenging for me.

It might be that those who used to stand alongside you have different reasons they have backed off now – but I imagine there are others in this room who know its harder to fight to spiritual growth now than it used to be because there are fewer friends willing to fight for growth with you now.

IN THE AREA OF PRACTICAL CHRISTIANITY

Joshua 24:14-15 KJV
Now therefore fear the LORD, and serve him in sincerity and in truth: and put away the gods which your fathers served on the other side of the flood, and in Egypt; and serve ye the LORD.
And if it seem evil unto you to serve the LORD, choose you this day whom ye will serve; whether the gods which your fathers served that were on the other side of the flood, or the gods of the Amorites, in whose land ye dwell: but as for me and my house, we will serve the LORD.

There is
- **Spiritual growth – coming to understand our faith -and then there is**
- **Practical growth - how we live out our faith**

In the letters of the Apostle Paul, you find a trend.
- **First Paul would teach a doctrinal truth**
- **Then Paul would explain how to live out that truth**

Spiritual growth would be akin to the doctrine. Practical Christianity would be akin to living out the truth. Practical Christianity amounts to things like:[4]

- **Husbands love your wives**
- **Wives submit to your husbands**
- **Children obey your parents**
- **Fathers provoke not your children**
- **Servants be obedient to your masters**
- **Masters do the same things to them**

Can anyone claim to have mastered any of these things?

IN THE AREA OF PERSONAL EVANGELISM

Joshua 10:6 KJV
And the men of Gibeon sent unto Joshua to the camp to Gilgal, saying, Slack not thy hand from thy servants; come up to us quickly, and save us, and help us: for all the kings of the Amorites that dwell in the mountains are gathered together against us.

I am reaching back too early in the history of Joshua's conquest of the Promised Land. Joshua had made a promise to a people known as the Gibeonites. They had really tricked him into the promise, but then there is one thing we can always be sure a sinner will do – they will sin.

The Bible says, Romans 5:8
But God commendeth His love toward us, in that, while we were yet sinners, Christ died for us.

Here are some sinners asking Joshua to come and save them. Can anyone claim that you are as successful in seeing souls saved as you ought to be?

There remaineth yet very much land to be possessed in this area of our faith, doesn't there?

- **When was the last time you purposely witnessed to another person?**
- **When did you give someone a gospel tract?**
- **When did you last invite someone to come to church with you?**

Is there any Christian excused from witnessing? Is there any excuse you believe will work when you stand before the Lord? No. The fact is, this is a piece of spiritual property we have all but given back to the enemy. It's a mountain, to be sure. We can't ever win a soul in our own strength. But:
- **the cause is just**
- **the need is urgent**
- **the call is still very much right**

Conclusion

The United States of America came finally to the place where they realized they could never remain free so long as they ignored that someone else in the world was not free. We could no longer have a strict isolationist doctrine. We had to fight so that others could be free.

God forbid that our church, that any of you, would embrace an isolationist position – refusing to fight for freedom
- **Freedom in personal spiritual growth**
- **Freedom in practical Christianity**
- **Freedom in personal evangelism**

[1] http://en.wikipedia.org/wiki/First_Barbary_War
[2] http://memory.loc.gov/ammem/collections/jefferson_papers/mtjprece.html
[3] Joshua being the other
[4] Ephesians 5:22-6:9

Chapter Five

FREE FOR ALL
Judges 21:25

I suppose it was natural that, in the decades just previous to the American Revolution, the subject of what it meant to be free was much discussed and studied. Thomas Paine, fresh off the boat from England, quickly bought into the spirit of liberty. James Madison, Thomas Jefferson, John Adams as well as the majority of the educated in America had been schooled in the history of the Roman Republic and in England's own John Locke. So it is no wonder that preachers were also tinkering in their heads and delivering from their pulpits ideas concerning liberty and what it means.

One of those men was Isaac Backus. I do not know that he was representative of what all Baptist preachers were thinking but he influences Baptist thinking today because he published what he wrote so we know what he thought. Prior to the Revolution, Backus was concerned about the spirit of rebellion he witnessed. Like the majority of the Baptists of his day he opposed the Revolutionary War, believing that what government might come out of it could be worse for religious liberty than what already existed. In a sermon that was primarily focused on pleading for individual soul liberty, Backus introduced the message with some thoughts concerning man, liberty and human governments. He knew that there was a need for law.

> "It is supposed by multitudes, that in submitting to government we give up some part of our liberty, because they imagine that there is something in their nature incompatible with each other. But the word of truth plainly shews, that

man first lost his freedom by breaking over the rules of government"

"What a dangerous error, yea what a root of all evil then it must be for men to imagine that there is anything in the nature of true government that interferes with true and full liberty!"
"We are not insensible that the general notion of liberty is for each one to act or conduct as he pleases; but that government obliges us to act toward others by law and rule, which in the imagination of many, interferes with such liberty; though when- we come- to the light of truth, what can possibly prevent it's being the highest pleasure, for every rational person, to love God with all his heart, and his neighbor as himself"[1]

Israel experienced a time in their history where they had no leadership, no restrictions and no laws. The Bible says it was a time when "there was no king in Israel: every man did what was right in his own eyes."

I remember the first time I read the book of Judges. There are some pretty dramatic stories of heroism and valor:

- **Ehud hiding a dagger in his clothing and killing the enemy king in his own tent**
- **Shamgar, single handedly killed 600 Philistines with just an ox goad, because he had no weapon**
- **Gideon and his 300 destroying the entire army of the Midianites**
- **Samson, blinded by his enemies, pushing a building down on himself and killing the enemies of Israel**

Some of the most fantastic miracles of the Bible happen in the days of the judges.

But the book of Judges is not a book about miracles – those miracles serve merely as a testimony of God's grace and mercy. The story of the book of Judges is a story of depravity. There are historical accounts in this book that are impossible to explain except that men, left to themselves – always sink into corruption and immorality.

And so, you have a traveler who, upon entering into a certain city of Israel, is attacked by the locals. To save himself, he gives them his concubine to abuse in any way they pleased and, when he finds her dead the next morning, hacks her body into twelve pieces and sends a piece to each of the tribes of Israel. Eleven of the twelve tribes respond in unbridled wrath and very nearly exterminate one whole tribe of God's chosen people.

You have the story of:
- **Deborah, a woman judge because there was no man who would be a man**
- **Samson the hero of Israel who died an ignominious death because he would not control his immorality**
- **Jephthah, the illegitimate son of Gideon who had to be talked into saving the Jews and then promised God to sacrifice the first person who walked in his door after the battle if he won the battle. He won and that person was his own daughter**

People constantly read these accounts and ask, "Why would God put stories like this in a book that is supposed to be all about His love and His desire to save people from hell?" The answer is straightforward and direct; these are recorded to illustrate what happens when people, even God's people, live without organized leadership – no law.

True Baptists believe that every human being has the absolute right to worship God according to the dictates of their own conscience. But that does not mean we believe in a spiritual free for all. I am not encouraging you to just do whatever you like about spiritual things:

- **Get saved if you like; don't be saved if you don't want to be**
- **Be scripturally baptized if it suits you; don't worry about it if baptism bothers you**
- **Attend church if you have the time; worship God fishing on the Sound if that is more inspiring to you**
- **Join the church that makes you feel good about yourself**
- **Pick whatever version of the Bible is easiest for you to leave on your coffee table because you don't have to read it unless you want to anyway**

Individual soul liberty is not interchangeable with doing what is right in your own eyes. Individual soul liberty expects that each man and each woman will reach out to the King of Kings and appeal to Him for direction guidance and rule in your life. As evil as a man might be without a king, he is far more evil without God.

Romans 1:28-29 KJV
And even as they did not like to retain God in their knowledge, God gave them over to a reprobate mind, to do those things which are not convenient;
Being filled with all unrighteousness, fornication, wickedness, covetousness, maliciousness; full of envy, murder, debate, deceit, malignity; whisperers,

The New Testament Christian is free.
John 8:32
And ye shall know the truth, and the truth shall make you free

But he is, nevertheless, under a law.
Romans 3:27 KJV
Where is boasting then? It is excluded. By what law? of works? Nay: but by the law of faith.

Romans 8:2 KJV

For the law of the Spirit of life in Christ Jesus hath made me free from the law of sin and death.

Let me give you four "principles of government" for the New Testament Christian. I am going to present them in the order in which they are given in the Bible.

A PRINCIPLE OF AUTHORITY

Matthew 18:17 KJV
And if he shall neglect to hear them, tell it unto the church: but if he neglect to hear the church, let him be unto thee as an heathen man and a publican.

Ever hear someone say that they do not like organized religion? What they think they mean by organized religion is "church". What they really mean is "authority". Jesus very clearly gave the church authority in matters of discipline.

1 Corinthians 6:1-5 KJV
Dare any of you, having a matter against another, go to law before the unjust, and not before the saints?
Do ye not know that the saints shall judge the world? and if the world shall be judged by you, are ye unworthy to judge the smallest matters?
Know ye not that we shall judge angels? how much more things that pertain to this life?
If then ye have judgments of things pertaining to this life, set them to judge who are least esteemed in the church.
I speak to your shame. Is it so, that there is not a wise man among you? no, not one that shall be able to judge between his brethren?

I know authority can be abused. It is what happened with the Catholics and Protestants who, having gained the authority of the state, began forcing spiritual rules on people. I deny that the government has any authority to make people believe anything or worship any particular way. But each local church does have authority to discipline its own members. I would rather lose members to some other body of so called Christians than lose that authority in the church. It is a voluntary authority to be sure. Each of us agrees to be under that authority when we unite with a particular church. But the authority does exist. To leave that church without the consent of the church is to be under immediate discipline of the church.

A PRINCIPLE OF ARRANGMENT

1 Corinthians 14:40 KJV
Let all things be done decently and in order.

1 Corinthians 12-14 is all about the local church. Paul concludes his arguments concerning the practice of spiritual gifts in the church by saying, "Let all things be done decently and in order." That means there is a certain format in the church. There are people in charge of various things in the church. Those people are in their place doing what it is they are responsible for. They do not try to take over and do someone else's work in the church. They do not step over the authorities in the church. They do not disrupt the sense of order and organization in the church. In other words no one is to come to church and do what is right in their own eyes. We each come to church and submit to the order that exists in the church.

A PRINCIPLE OF ACTION

1 Timothy 3:15 KJV
But if I tarry long, that thou mayest know how thou oughtest to behave thyself in the house of God, which is the church of the living God, the pillar and ground of the truth.

The key word in this verse, for the purpose of this message, is "behave". There is a proper behavior for members of a local church.
- **It is a way that is helpful to the members of the church[2]**
- **It is a way that is humble and prefers others before ourselves[3]**

- **It is a way that is honest both inside the church house and out[4]**
- **It is a way that is honoring to the Lord Jesus Christ[5]**

Paul summed all of this up with Ephesians 4:1 KJV
I therefore, the prisoner of the Lord, beseech you that ye walk worthy of the vocation wherewith ye are called,

No Christian, regardless of the liberty they perceive themselves to have, ought to behave in a way that is beneath the person of the Lord Jesus Christ.

A PRINCIPLE OF ASSEMBLING

Hebrews 10:24-26 KJV
And let us consider one another to provoke unto love and to good works:
Not forsaking the assembling of ourselves together, as the manner of some is; but exhorting one another: and so much the more, as ye see the day approaching.
For if we sin wilfully after that we have received the knowledge of the truth, there remaineth no more sacrifice for sins,

I think it is important to put these three verses together because we see in verse 24 a motive for not forsaking our attendance to church services – to be a help to others and we see in verse 26 a result in not forsaking attendance to church services – it helps to prevent willful sin.

Have you ever heard that phrase "Ignorance of the law is no excuse"? Nowhere is that more true than concerning the law of the spirit of life in Christ Jesus.
- **Unlike the laws of men, His law never changes**
- **We have an infallible and preserved book that records that law and**
- **He has built His church as a place where we can learn that law**

Conclusion

It is significant that the "heroes" of the book of Judges are all called judges. Every revival of Jewish spiritual and national life during that period of their history centered around someone whose role was to restore order and law. When the majority of the people were united around a rule of law, they had revival. Let me tell you why YOU ought to want to be a part of the revival of spiritual law in your life and why it is important to urge Christians to reject "free for all" Christianity. Without submission to the "law of the spirit of life in Christ Jesus" a lost person:

- **your husband**
- **your wife**
- **your son**
- **your daughter**
- **your neighbor**
- **your best friend**

will never see a path that leads to salvation. If we all are only doing what is right in our own eyes, there is no reason he or she should not do what is right in his or her eyes. Only when we follow the law will they be able to see our King.

[1] Isaac Backus, An Appeal to the Public for Religious Liberty against the Oppressions of the Present Day, iBooks

[2] 1 Corinthians 10:23 KJV

All things are lawful for me, but all things are not expedient: all things are lawful for me, but all things edify not.

[3] Philippians 2:3 KJV

Let nothing be done through strife or vainglory; but in lowliness of mind let each esteem other better than themselves.

[4] Romans 12:17 KJV

Recompense to no man evil for evil. Provide things honest in the sight of all men.

[5] Philippians 1:27 KJV

Only let your conversation be as it becometh the gospel of Christ: that whether I come and see you, or else be absent, I may hear of your affairs, that ye stand fast in one spirit, with one mind striving together for the faith of the gospel;

Chapter Six

A TALE OF TWO KINGDOMS
1 Samuel 13:1-14 KJV

Saul reigned one year; and when he had reigned two years over Israel, Saul chose him three thousand men of Israel; whereof two thousand were with Saul in Michmash and in mount Bethel, and a thousand were with Jonathan in Gibeah of Benjamin: and the rest of the people he sent every man to his tent.

And Jonathan smote the garrison of the Philistines that was in Geba, and the Philistines heard of it. And Saul blew the trumpet throughout all the land, saying, Let the Hebrews hear.

And all Israel heard say that Saul had smitten a garrison of the Philistines, and that Israel also was had in abomination with the Philistines. And the people were called together after Saul to Gilgal.

And the Philistines gathered themselves together to fight with Israel, thirty thousand chariots, and six thousand horsemen, and people as the sand which is on the sea shore in multitude: and they came up, and pitched in Michmash, eastward from Beth-aven.

When the men of Israel saw that they were in a strait, (for the people were distressed,) then the people did hide themselves in caves, and in thickets, and in rocks, and in high places, and in pits.

And some of the Hebrews went over Jordan to the land of Gad and Gilead. As for Saul, he was yet in Gilgal, and all the people followed him trembling.

And he tarried seven days, according to the set time that Samuel had appointed: but Samuel came not to Gilgal; and the people were scattered from him.

And Saul said, Bring hither a burnt-offering to me, and peace-offerings. And he offered the burnt-offering.

And it came to pass, that as soon as he had made an end of offering the burnt- offering, behold, Samuel came; and Saul went out to meet him, that he might salute him.

And Samuel said, What hast thou done? And Saul said, Because I saw that the people were scattered from me, and that thou camest not within the days appointed, and that the Philistines gathered themselves together at Michmash;

Therefore said I, The Philistines will come down now upon me to Gilgal, and I have not made supplication unto the LORD: I forced myself therefore, and offered a burnt-offering.

And Samuel said to Saul, Thou hast done foolishly: thou hast not kept the commandment of the LORD thy God, which he commanded thee: for now would the LORD have established thy kingdom upon Israel for ever.

But now thy kingdom shall not continue: the LORD hath sought him a man after his own heart, and the LORD hath commanded him to be captain over his people, because thou hast not kept that which the LORD commanded thee.

One of the great fears everyone had just prior to and up through the ratifying of the Constitution of the United States was that of, if we were no longer under British rule, what kind of rule would replace her? Americans were, for the most part, proud citizens of England and that despite her flaws. There were much worse systems of government out there:

- **There were despots**
- **There were tyrants**
- **There were absolute monarchs**

Peter the Great, of Russia, had lived just 100 years previous and, though a member of the Enlightenment, he was such a cruel man that he personally supervised the torture of his own son.

England was considered the envy of Europe because, though she had a Monarchy, it was a limited monarchy. The people prided themselves in ruling themselves. What if that was lost in the struggle to gain independence from England? Baptists, Quakers, Plymouth Brethren and other smaller Christian groups initially opposed the Revolution, taking the more conservative, "better to keep what we know we have than fight for, we know not what we will have" position. But even the aggressive "Sons of Liberty" were very fearful of giving power to any one person. Independent and local militia fired the first few volleys of the American Revolution. When the Continental Congress finally did appoint a Commander in Chief of the Continental Armies, they did so with some trepidation and for the first part of the War maintained much of the authority over Washington. Their reasoning was simple. They knew that the man who controlled that powerful an army could easily promote himself to king – or worse.

After the Revolution was won, though there was still an acting Continental Congress, the ultimate powers rested in the Constitutions of each state. When it became obvious to many that the United States could not long survive without a much stronger federal government, years worth of debates ensued over whether we should have a stronger federal government, and if so, what kind of government should it be? Alexander Hamilton championed something akin to a monarchy. He believed that the only stable government would be one bordering on absolute power. Thomas Jefferson took the opposite position. He believed that each generation (he defined that as about 17 years) should have their own revolution and write their own Constitution.

When the men who finally served to create our Constitution of the United States of America sealed themselves in that room in Philadelphia, their desire was to establish a system of government, not after their own choosing but of God's. During a particularly difficult time in the Constitutional Convention, James Madison wrote in his notes on the Convention that Benjamin Franklin appealed to the delegates and said;

> "In the beginning of the Contest with G. Britain, when we were sensible of danger we had daily prayer in this room for the divine protection. - Our prayers, Sir, were heard, & they were graciously answered. All of us who were engaged in the struggle must have observed frequent

instances of a superintending providence in our favor.

To that kind providence we owe this happy opportunity of consulting in peace on the means of establishing our future national felicity. And have we now forgotten that powerful friend? or do we imagine that we no longer need his assistance? I have lived, Sir, a long time, and the longer I live, the more convincing proofs I see of this truth- that God Governs in the affairs of men. And if a sparrow cannot fall to the ground without his notice, is it probable that an empire can rise without his aid? We have been assured, Sir, in the sacred writings, that "except the Lord build the House they labour in vain that build it." I firmly believe this; and I also believe that without his concurring aid we shall succeed in this political building no better, than the Builders of Babel:"

Israel found themselves in a very trying situation.
- **Joshua was dead**
- **The Judges had been sporadic at best**
- **Every man doing what was right in his own eyes was a disaster**

Something HAD to change, and they knew it. But a government is nothing to be taken on lightly.

When the Jews first approached their prophet Samuel and demanded of him, 1 Samuel 8:5-6 KJV
... make us a king to judge us like all the nations.

The thing displeased Samuel and he warned them.
1 Samuel 8:11-18 KJV
And he said, This will be the manner of the king that shall reign over you: He will take your sons, and appoint them for himself, for his

chariots, and to be his horsemen; and some shall run before his chariots.

And he will appoint him captains over thousands, and captains over fifties; and will set them to ear his ground, and to reap his harvest, and to make his instruments of war, and instruments of his chariots.

And he will take your daughters to be confectionaries, and to be cooks, and to be bakers.

And he will take your fields, and your vineyards, and your oliveyards, even the best of them, and give them to his servants.

And he will take the tenth of your seed, and of your vineyards, and give to his officers, and to his servants.

And he will take your menservants, and your maidservants, and your goodliest young men, and your asses, and put them to his work.

He will take the tenth of your sheep: and ye shall be his servants.

And ye shall cry out in that day because of your king which ye shall have chosen you; and the LORD will not hear you in that day.

What follows is what I am going to call, "The Tale of Two Kingdoms".

A KING OF MAN'S OWN CHOOSING

1 Samuel 10:17-23 KJV

And Samuel called the people together unto the LORD to Mizpeh;

And said unto the children of Israel, Thus saith the LORD God of Israel, I brought up Israel out of Egypt, and delivered you out of the hand of the Egyptians, and out of the hand of all kingdoms, and of them that oppressed you:

And ye have this day rejected your God, who himself saved you out of all your adversities and your tribulations; and ye have said unto him, Nay, but set a king over us. Now therefore present yourselves before the LORD by your tribes, and by your thousands.

And when Samuel had caused all the tribes of Israel to come near, the tribe of Benjamin was taken.

When he had caused the tribe of Benjamin to come near by their families, the family of Matri was taken, and Saul the son of Kish was taken: and when they sought him, he could not be found.

Therefore they enquired of the LORD further, if the man should yet come thither. And the LORD answered, Behold, he hath hid himself among the stuff.
And they ran and fetched him thence: and when he stood among the people, he was higher than any of the people from his shoulders and upward.

For those sticklers to detail, I readily admit that it was God who told Samuel about Saul, but it was the people who demanded that they be given a king.

Saul, Israel's first king is a type of Satan
The things we know about Saul:
- **He started out well – a very pleasing looking choice for king**
- **He became lifted up in pride**
- **He took too much upon himself**
- **He became jealous of God's will**
- **He attacked the will of God**
- **He ended in terrible defeat**

Satan
- **Began as Lucifer, the highest of God's angels**
- **Lifted himself up in pride**
- **Said he would become like the most high God**
- **Opposes Christ and all who follow Him**
- **Will end finally in the bottomless pit**

Saul looked just like they imagined their ideal king would look.
- **He was tall**
- **He seemed to be humble**
- **He acted spiritual**

But the truth was that he was:
- **Self-willed**
- **Self-centered**
- **Abusive**

You and I will be ruled by one of two "kingdoms"
- **The flesh**
- **The Spirit**[1]

We were born under the dominion of the flesh. The Psalmist said, *"Behold, I was shapen in iniquity; and in sin did my mother conceive me."[[2]]* Following the rule of our flesh can be very appealing at first:
- **It's handy since it is already installed as king of our life**
- **It gives instant gratification**
- **It delivers to us a sense of pride – its part of who we are**
- **It is logical. We can define it since we see it**

On the other hand, King Flesh ends very poorly. The Bible says; *"sin, when it is finished, bringeth forth death."*[3]

A KING OF GOD'S CHOOSING

1 Samuel 13:13-14 KJV

And Samuel said to Saul, Thou hast done foolishly: thou hast not kept the commandment of the LORD thy God, which he commanded thee: for now would the LORD have established thy kingdom upon Israel for ever.

But now thy kingdom shall not continue: the LORD hath sought him a man after his own heart, and the LORD hath commanded him to be captain over his people, because thou hast not kept that which the LORD commanded thee.

King David is a type of Christ
- **Began as a lowly shepherd**
- **Fought for his people before he was anything in their eyes**
- **Was first a servant long before He was a king**
- **Persecuted by Saul (Satan)**
- **Patient before assuming authority**
- **Sacrificed himself before sending anyone to battle**

Jesus Christ
- **Was born in a lowly manger**

- Lived His early years in a carpenter's house
- Suffered the very probably death of His step father Joseph
- Lived a sinless and righteous life
- Performed many helpful and healing miracles but was
- Hated by the Jews
- Killed though they knew He was innocent

Before Jesus died He promised us that He would not leave us comfortless but that He would send a Comforter, the Holy Spirit of God. And now, anyone who asks is born again.

- Christ becomes his or her king
- The Spirit of God takes up home inside of him
- The Spirit of God becomes his new guide in life

I will confess that the rule of the Holy Spirit has some challenges:

- It is contrary to our old nature
- It is spiritual and not physical
- It is discouraged by most of our friends and family
- We are taught it is superstition in our educational system
- It will almost certainly bring with it some persecution

But this kingdom provides for us:

- Purpose for life today
- Joy and peace of mind in trials and
- Eternal life and rewards in the future

For a time the Jews had,

TWO KINGS AND TWO KINGDOMS

In the days of the kings
The citizens were:
1. Divided
King Saul was the apparent power.

- He had precedent

- **He had an army**
- **He had on the crown**

King David on the other hand, worked for King Saul, had been secretly anointed king and was still young. He was popular and he was a war hero; but was he really powerful enough to overthrow King Saul. And then there was the whole fact that he would not even try to overthrow King Saul.

And so it was that it was only the,

2. Minority with David
1 Samuel 22:2 KJV

And every one that was in distress, and every one that was in debt, and every one that was discontented, gathered themselves unto him; and he became a captain over them: and there were with him about four hundred men.

Though King David's numbers steadily grew, Saul always had the majority.

Once King Saul died and David was the king of the whole nation, his followers were:

3. Easily swept back to the fleshly king
Saul was dead.

- **But Ishbosheth, his son was still alive and they supported him while they could**
- **When Absalom rebels against his dad, the Saul loyalists automatically supported him**
- **After Solomon died, the kingdom split again into those who were true to David and those who would have been initially true to Saul**

The minority stuck to God's leadership. The majority kept drifting back into following the flesh. And so it is still today. Jesus said, Matthew 7:13-14 KJV

Enter ye in at the strait gate: for wide is the gate, and broad is the way, that leadeth to destruction, and many there be which go in thereat:

Because strait is the gate, and narrow is the way, which leadeth unto life, and few there be that find it.

Our world is divided between those who earnestly wish to follow the Spirit of God and those who, even while often claiming to be spiritual people, naturally tend to follow the flesh. And the majority always follow the flesh.

- **There is a way – a kingdom – that leads to destruction**
- **There is another way – a kingdom – that leads to eternal life**

If you want to follow that way that leads to eternal life and rewards in eternal life, you are going to have to choose the unnatural way, you will need to do the unnatural thing. You will need to call out to Christ for salvation first of all. Then you will need to die to your flesh daily so that Christ lives in you.

Which kingdom will you choose?

[1] Galatians 5:16 KJV
This I say then, Walk in the Spirit, and ye shall not fulfil the lust of the flesh.
[2] Psalm 51:5
[3] James 1:15

Chapter Seven

SACRIFICE AND HEARTACHE; THE STEPPINGSTONES TO LIBERTY

2 Samuel 21:15-21 KJV

Moreover the Philistines had yet war again with Israel; and David went down, and his servants with him, and fought against the Philistines: and David waxed faint.

And Ishbi-benob, which was of the sons of the giant, the weight of whose spear weighed three hundred shekels of brass in weight, he being girded with a new sword, thought to have slain David.

But Abishai the son of Zeruiah succoured him, and smote the Philistine, and killed him. Then the men of David sware unto him, saying, Thou shalt go no more out with us to battle, that thou quench not the light of Israel.

And it came to pass after this, that there was again a battle with the Philistines at Gob: then Sibbechai the Hushathite slew Saph, which was of the sons of the giant.

And there was again a battle in Gob with the Philistines, where Elhanan the son of Jaare-oregim, a Beth=lehemite, slew the brother of Goliath the Gittite, the staff of whose spear was like a weaver's beam.

And there was yet a battle in Gath, where was a man of great stature, that had on every hand six fingers, and on every foot six toes, four and twenty in number; and he also was born to the giant.

And when he defied Israel, Jonathan the son of Shimea the brother of David slew him.

I read one time about an account of the fateful moment General Dwight Eisenhower gave the final order to begin the invasion of Normandy, code named "Operation Overlord". I understand that, as the final preparations were being made, Eisenhower was advised that up to 70% of the invasion forces could be killed. In his memoirs he later wrote that, "He feared that he "would carry to [his] grave the unbearable burden of a conscience justly accusing [him] of the stupid, blind sacrifice of thousands of flower of our youth"[1] The plans for Operation Overlord depended heavily on weather and tide conditions.

Neither seemed like they were helping the Allied cause. June 5 was the original launch date but, when weather prevented that, Eisenhower thought they might have to wait until the 18th. They were already having trouble with information leaks and things of that nature so that, when it was suggested the June 6 offered acceptable conditions, Eisenhower gave the order with three simple words, "Okay, Let's go." And the invasion was executed. Liberty never comes without great sacrifice and, often, incredible heartache.

Doesn't it always seem like just when you get on a roll to do the right thing, something happens to try to get you off track? Your own fight for spiritual liberty comes with sacrifice and often with much heartache.

Israel has experienced the very same thing throughout their history. From the moment they left the slavery of Egypt, it seemed like there was always someone else wanting to capture and enslave them.
- **It is true throughout the Bible era**
- **It is true even today**

- **In the days of the wilderness, it was the Amalekites**
- **In the days of the judges, it was the Midianites**
- **In the early days of the Kings, it was the Philistines**

I want to focus on just one family of those Philistines. Those Philistines in Gath were a particular thorn in David's kingdom. There is first of all,

AN ARMY STOPPING GIANT

1 Samuel 17:4 KJV

And there went out a champion out of the camp of the Philistines, named Goliath, of Gath, whose height was six cubits and a span.

A. Admittedly, Goliath has some army stopping qualities.
* He is big
* He is threatening
* He is blasphemous

I can understand why they are having some difficulty finding someone to answer his challenge. This is a bad dude! And the way Goliath is presenting himself, all the stakes lie in this one contest.
- **If Goliath wins Israel serve the Philistines**
- **If the Israelite wins, the Philistines serve Israel**

But I have a couple of questions:
- **Why doesn't the army just go stomp on him?**
- **Who made the rule that one of their guys had to fight him?**

Where did we ever get the idea that Christianity has to fit nicely within the world's rules?
- **I am not talking about breaking the laws of the land**
- **I am talking about embracing the world's traditions and culture as our own**

We ought to be different; markedly so.

Here enters David.
B. He breaks all of the acceptable rules of war in his time:
- **He is too young**
- **He does not wear armor**
- **He does not carry a conventional weapon**
- **He calls on the name of the Lord as His help**

And then,
- **He slays Goliath with His own sword**

C. The Bible is to be the Christians only rule of faith and practice
And it is the Bible alone that we ought to allow to place expectations on us. Even inside the church –

- **This is not a place where we force each other to comply with the expectations of the congregation**
- **This is a place where we have agreed together to come learn what are God's expectations for His people**

Considering David's experience with Goliath of Gath, it is shocking to see that his next contact with them is as:

A COMPROMISING KING

1 Samuel 27:1-2 KJV

And David said in his heart, I shall now perish one day by the hand of Saul: there is nothing better for me than that I should speedily escape into the land of the Philistines; and Saul shall despair of me, to seek me any more in any coast of Israel: so shall I escape out of his hand.
And David arose, and he passed over with the six hundred men that were with him unto Achish, the son of Maoch, king of Gath.

I have a Bible at home called the Classic King James Bible. It's title for 1 Samuel 27 is, "David's Lapse of Faith. He goes to Philistia".

Perhaps one of the most dangerous times in the history of Israel was when the man who had been anointed king chose to go live with the enemy.
- **These were sworn enemies of the Jews**
- **David's presence in no way altered**
- **David was even expected to fight against the Jews**

Wouldn't it be easy to think that David was justified in going to Gath?
- **His own king was trying to kill him**
- **No matter where he went in Israel, the king was sure to have spies**
- **Anyone in Israel who was friendly with him was at risk of execution**

And here was the enemy – willing to welcome him into their camp.

The very nature of compromise is that it looks justifiable. That is the danger of it. It can seem like the right thing to do, the only thing to do. But friendship with this world is always enmity with God. Always. That's why for nearly 1600 years Christians died rather than compromise with Catholics and Protestant churches. They saw that the little bits of leaven in what looked like an otherwise decent sack of flour, had in fact leavened the whole lump.

The trouble with compromise with the world is that the world never compromises. The King of Gath, never changed his agenda to attack and plunder Israel, did he? He accepted David only because he expected David to embrace his agenda, even in attacking Israel with him. Remember this, Christian, the world will never truly accept your faith. It might tolerate it for a while, but eventually it will expect you to side with it. It might not be you who pays the price of that compromise. It might be your children or your grandchildren, but eventually the world will expect (require) you to join them in hating the faith.

David's third encounter with Gath is when he was,

OLDER AND OUTNUMBERED

2 Samuel 21:20 KJV
And there was yet a battle in Gath, where was a man of great stature, that had on every hand six fingers, and on every foot six toes, four and twenty in number; and he also was born to the giant.

Though David had fallen in his faith, God was not finished with him. Eventually David saw the compromise for what it was and made a clean break from Gath. He went on to become the King of all of Israel and to become the enemy of Gath once again. David and his armies fought the Philistines and Gath the rest of their lives.

Galatians 5:1 KJV says,
Stand fast therefore in the liberty wherewith Christ hath made us free, and be not entangled again with the yoke of bondage.

The reason you have to stand fast in your liberty is because the world, the flesh and the devil are never going to quit trying to take it from you. This is a lifelong fight. We never get to:
- **Declare a truce**
- **Sign a peace treaty**

There will never be
- **An armistice**
- **Detente**
- **Peace Initiative**

You know what happens when we fight for a long time, don't you? You get tired. You get weary in well doing. You get faint in the battle. Years ago, I purchased a book by a Fundamental Baptist preacher from down south somewhere. The book's title was, *Dear Preacher, Please Quit.* The premise of the book was that, too often, preachers, who have fought the battle of faith for two or three or four decades, just give up the fight. He said that if you are going to give up, you ought to go ahead and quit – let someone who will do the battle step in.

I sat down, maybe twenty years ago with a couple of preachers fifteen to twenty years my senior. They were reminiscing about the early days of Fundamental Baptist Churches and how they stood for
- **Doctrines**
- **Righteousness**
- **Convictions**

One of the two had been an assistant pastor at a church whose pastor was famous for his powerful ministry. But as the years had gone by, this pastor and that church had slowly stopped standing where they once were.

- **The pastor stopped insisting on Baptist baptism only**
- **The pastor stopped standing for Lord's Supper for members only**

The church began to drift on standards of dress and Christian conduct so that, by the time I became a preacher, this once famous church now pastored by the famous preacher's son, is considered one of the most liberal churches in Fundamental Baptist history. I asked this preacher I was having lunch with what happened. He said he had asked the once powerful preacher the same question. His answer to him was, "Ron, I just got tired of the fight."

Not five years ago I sat at a meal with a man, now out of the ministry, who had trained under one of Texas' most well known Baptist preachers. That preacher has resigned his church and now teaches at one of the more liberal Fundamental Baptist Colleges in our country. This guy called up his pastor and asked him why he had made the switch. His answer was, "I just got tired." The guy I was speaking to then said, "If my pastor can get tired and quit, so can I." And he did.

Now those are preachers. But they are not the only ones who grow weary and quit. I have witnessed Christians on all levels do that very same thing. They just get tired of standing up against:

- **The world**
- **The devil**
- **Their flesh**

Now, I could give you all sorts of proposed antidotes for growing weary"
- **Get a prayer partner**
- **Counsel with your pastor**
- **Think of the testimony for your children**
-

But the Bible doesn't really give us those antidotes. The Bible says just don't let it happen:
- **Be not weary in well doing**
- **Stand Fast therefore**

And that is where I want to end, Galatians 5:1 KJV,
Stand fast therefore in the liberty wherewith Christ hath made us free, and be not entangled again with the yoke of bondage.

There will be sacrifice and there will be heartache in your struggle for spiritual liberty. Take heart! They are merely steppingstones on your way to freedom.

[1] http://ww2db.com/battle_spec.php?battle_id=2, accessed 4-9-15

Chapter Eight

ARNOLD

1 Kings 2:1-6 KJV
Now the days of David drew nigh that he should die; and he charged Solomon his son, saying,
I go the way of all the earth: be thou strong therefore, and shew thyself a man;
And keep the charge of the LORD thy God, to walk in his ways, to keep his statutes, and his commandments, and his judgments, and his testimonies, as it is written in the law of Moses, that thou mayest prosper in all that thou doest, and whithersoever thou turnest thyself:
That the LORD may continue his word which he spake concerning me, saying, If thy children take heed to their way, to walk before me in truth with all their heart and with all their soul, there shall not fail thee (said he) a man on the throne of Israel.
Moreover thou knowest also what Joab the son of Zeruiah did to me, and what he did to the two captains of the hosts of Israel, unto Abner the son of Ner, and unto Amasa the son of Jether, whom he slew, and shed the blood of war in peace, and put the blood of war upon his girdle that was about his loins, and in his shoes that were on his feet.
Do therefore according to thy wisdom, and let not his hoar head go down to the grave in peace.

Early on in the war for our country's independence from England a shining star rose to the front. Benedict Arnold had become an American hero. He helped defeat Ft. Ticonderoga. The victory won gave Washington the canons much needed to liberate Boston Harbor. Later, Arnold, not a sailing man himself, built a navy on Lake Champlain. He lost the naval battles but bought time the Americans needed to defend Ft. Ticonderoga from the British attempt to retake it. He was wounded twice – once in an attempt to take the city of Quebec and again at Saratoga

Arnold had served so admirably that he was General Washington's most trusted officer; his "go to" man. To shift illustrations for a moment, Arnold would have been to Washington what Stonewall Jackson was to General Robert E Lee. When Jackson sustained the wound that eventually cost him his life, his left arm had to be amputated, Lee's comment was, "Jackson has lost his left arm. But I have lost my right." Arnold was Washington's right arm man. Some historians believe that, if there had been no Benedict Arnold, there would be no America. His exploits were monumental in the fight for liberty. It would have been easier on General Washington if he had died in battle than that he had turned traitor.

But the Devil had been at work in Arnold for some time:
- **He had a scuffle with Ethan Allen and the Green Mountain Boys over who was in charge at Ticonderoga**
- **He was miffed that he had not been (in his mind) recognized for his valor**
- **He was jealous that he had been passed up for promotion by the Continental Congress**
- **He was involved with a woman who turned out to be a traitor in her own right**

For these and who knows how many other reasons, Arnold attempted to deliver West Point to the British. This act of treason was taken so harshly by Washington that it nearly put him in a tailspin of depression. No wonder that congress passed a law that the name of Benedict Arnold may be neither chiseled in stone or cast in metal. George Washington wanted his name to be forever banished from our memories and decreed that no written history of the Revolutionary War include the name Benedict Arnold. Washington was crushed by his treason.

King David reigned during what was arguably the height of Jewish Liberty. His was, no doubt, an era of war, but there was never before or since a King in Israel who so longed for his people to know and walk with God. His kingdom was certainly not perfect nor was David a perfect man. But he was a man after God's own heart.[1] David had his own Benedict Arnold. King David's Arnold was named Joab. He too was a notable hero, but he like Arnold, had personal demons that drove him to break the heart of David and eventually lead to his execution by King Solomon.

Amazingly, the names of Joab's four demons all began with the same letter.

ABNER

2 Samuel 3:23-30 KJV
When Joab and all the host that was with him were come, they told Joab, saying, Abner the son of Ner came to the king, and he hath sent him away, and he is gone in peace.
Then Joab came to the king, and said, What hast thou done? behold, Abner came unto thee; why is it that thou hast sent him away, and he is quite gone?
Thou knowest Abner the son of Ner, that he came to deceive thee, and to know thy going out and thy coming in, and to know all that thou doest.
And when Joab was come out from David, he sent messengers after Abner, which brought him again from the well of Sirah: but David knew it not.
And when Abner was returned to Hebron, Joab took him aside in the gate to speak with him quietly, and smote him there under the fifth rib, that he died, for the blood of Asahel his brother.
And afterward when David heard it, he said, I and my kingdom are guiltless before the LORD for ever from the blood of Abner the son of Ner:
Let it rest on the head of Joab, and on all his father's house; and let there not fail from the house of Joab one that hath an issue, or that is a leper, or that leaneth on a staff, or that falleth on the sword, or that lacketh bread.
So Joab and Abishai his brother slew Abner, because he had slain their brother Asahel at Gibeon in the battle.

Abner was King Saul's commander in chief but when Saul died[2] Abner began talks to bring unity into the kingdom. Trouble was, that before his realization, he had killed Joab's brother, Asahel. Abner had killed Asahel in combat, but Joab murdered Abner.

Joab's demon was not Abner – it was revenge. Bitterness over the death of his brother had so rotted his heart that he could not see that God had changed the heart of Abner. This man, who had once been the enemy of David, could have been the instrument of God to restore the people of God.

Is there any bitterness in your heart?
- **Has someone hurt you so badly you can't see any possibility of good in them?**
- **Have you become so spoiled through bitterness that you would let rip apart the will of God rather than rejoice in reconciliation?**

Years ago, I experienced one of the most unbelievable moments of restoration I could have ever imagined. I had preached at a rescue mission and a man there got saved. Afterwards I encouraged him to come to church the next Sunday and be baptized. He did. At the end of the service one of the men of the church came to me. He was white and trembling. He told me that the man I had just baptized had murdered his sister-in-law years previous and that the last thing he told her family when they sentenced him to prison was that he would kill them if he ever got out. The man from my church was obvious shaken but:
- **The guy I baptized was sincerely repentant**
- **The man in my church (and his family) forgave him**

Demon number one is revenge.

Demon two focuses around

ABSALOM

2 Samuel 18:5-14 KJV

And the king commanded Joab and Abishai and Ittai, saying, Deal gently for my sake with the young man, even with Absalom. And all the people heard when the king gave all the captains charge concerning Absalom.

So the people went out into the field against Israel: and the battle was in the wood of Ephraim;

Where the people of Israel were slain before the servants of David, and there was there a great slaughter that day of twenty thousand men.

For the battle was there scattered over the face of all the country: and the wood devoured more people that day than the sword devoured.

And Absalom met the servants of David. And Absalom rode upon a mule, and the mule went under the thick boughs of a great oak, and his head caught hold of the oak, and he was taken up between the heaven and the earth; and the mule that was under him went away.

And a certain man saw it, and told Joab, and said, Behold, I saw Absalom hanged in an oak.

And Joab said unto the man that told him, And, behold, thou sawest him, and why didst thou not smite him there to the ground? and I would have given thee ten shekels of silver, and a girdle.

And the man said unto Joab, Though I should receive a thousand shekels of silver in mine hand, yet would I not put forth mine hand against the king's son: for in our hearing the king charged thee and Abishai and Ittai, saying, Beware that none touch the young man Absalom.

Otherwise I should have wrought falsehood against mine own life: for there is no matter hid from the king, and thou thyself wouldest have set thyself against me.

Then said Joab, I may not tarry thus with thee. And he took three darts in his hand, and thrust them through the heart of Absalom, while he was yet alive in the midst of the oak.

As I said, King David was not perfect and one of the areas his imperfections most clearly showed up was in his children. Absalom was one of King David's own children and was a very troubled young man.

It is not my purpose to rehearse his life for you, but his last troubled act was to lead a rebellion against his father. He almost succeeded too. David was forced to flee the city of Jerusalem and a battle between the rebels and David's own men was fought. His soldiers urged King David not to go into battle himself. David agreed but insisted that his son Absalom not be slain in the combat.

- **Everyone heard**
- **Joab heard**

But when word came to Joab that Absalom had gotten trapped, hanging by his hair in a tree, ignoring the King's command, Joab rushed to the scene and put three darts into Absalom's heart.

In this case Joab's demon was recklessness; absolute disregard for the command of his superior.

One of the most common demons in the Christian world today is this demon of recklessness. Too many Christians, including those who claim to be leaders in churches – pastors, deacons, Sunday school teachers; choose to disregard what they have been taught – believing they know what is best.

Christians who know better drinking alcohol and flaunting that they do so:

- **Disregard for standards of modesty**
- **Disregard for separation from worldliness**
- **Disregard for doctrine and righteousness**

Joab's first demon was revenge
Joab's second demon was recklessness

The third demon centered around

AMASA

2 Samuel 20:9-13 KJV

And Joab said to Amasa, Art thou in health, my brother? And Joab took Amasa by the beard with the right hand to kiss him.

But Amasa took no heed to the sword that was in Joab's hand: so he smote him therewith in the fifth rib, and shed out his bowels to the ground, and struck him not again; and he died. So Joab and Abishai his brother pursued after Sheba the son of Bichri.

And one of Joab's men stood by him, and said, He that favoureth Joab, and he that is for David, let him go after Joab.

And Amasa wallowed in blood in the midst of the highway. And when the man saw that all the people stood still, he removed Amasa out of the highway into the field, and cast a cloth upon him, when he saw that every one that came by him stood still.

When he was removed out of the highway, all the people went on after Joab, to pursue after Sheba the son of Bichri.

Once again, Joab murdered a man in cold blood. Remember, King David has no reason to really trust Joab. He is a powerful warrior without question, but he is also a loose cannon. David could not be reasonably expected to make Joab his own Commander in Chief. He won't follow orders unless those orders make sense to Joab. So David promoted Amasa and ordered him to see to a rebellion led by a man named Sheba.

Turns out Amasa was a poor general, but without David's consent, Joab put together his own strike team, killed Amasa and then defeated Sheba.

In this case Joab's demon was rivalry, we might know it better as jealousy. He killed Amasa because Amasa had the recognition he wanted.

Turns out jealousy was the demon that defeated Benedict Arnold too.

- **He was a hero at Ticonderoga, but never got recognized for it**

- **It was his idea to march on Montreal, but Schuyler and Montgomery were put in charge and not him**
- **He was passed up for promotions he thought he deserved**

Rivalry – Jealousy.

- **Someone else gets recognition you think you deserve**
- **Someone else gets a position you really wanted**
- **Someone else gets to own something and you do not**
- **Someone else has an easier life than you have**
- **Someone else makes more money than you make**

It can be something trivial and small, it doesn't have to be a huge thing. But someone else has it and not you. And you grow to hate them for it.

Joab, ever a man after his own advancement and not that of the kingdom, tried to replace King Solomon with another of David's sons' Adonijah. King David's dying charge to Solomon was that Joab be slain for his fourth demon; rebellion. Joab fled to the altar at Gibeon where he was slain. His demons, in the end, destroyed him.

Conclusion

Benedict Arnold and his wife Peggy lived out the remainder of their lives in England. For their part in turning against the Americans, the British government provided the two of them a living until their deaths in 1802. But Benedict Arnold was never accepted by the Brits. They all knew he was a traitor.

On his deathbed Arnold requested that he be dressed in his old Continental uniform and said, "Let me die in this old uniform in which I fought my battles. May God forgive me for ever having put on another."[3]

Are any of these "demons" robbing you of the liberty wherewith Christ hath made us free?[4]

[1] I think he sought after God's heart.
[2] And after realizing that Ishbosheth, Saul's son, was a poor choice as king of Israel.
[3] This may be a legend.
[4] Galatians 5:1 KJV
STAND fast therefore in the liberty wherewith Christ hath made us free, and be not entangled again with the yoke of bondage.

Chapter Nine

THEY WILL FIGHT

2 Samuel 23:8-12 KJV

These be the names of the mighty men whom David had: The Tachmonite that sat in the seat, chief among the captains; the same was Adino the Eznite: he lift up his spear against eight hundred, whom he slew at one time.

And after him was Eleazar the son of Dodo the Ahohite, one of the three mighty men with David, when they defied the Philistines that were there gathered together to battle, and the men of Israel were gone away:

He arose, and smote the Philistines until his hand was weary, and his hand clave unto the sword: and the LORD wrought a great victory that day; and the people returned after him only to spoil.

And after him was Shammah the son of Agee the Hararite. And the Philistines were gathered together into a troop, where was a piece of ground full of lentiles: and the people fled from the Philistines.

But he stood in the midst of the ground, and defended it, and slew the Philistines: and the LORD wrought a great victory.

June of 1775 American Colonialists had received word that the British were planning to capture Boston's high ground at Dorchester Heights and Charlestown. One thousand, two hundred Colonialists led by a man named William Prescott, rushed to the scene and overnight constructed defensive works on a hill called Breed's Hill. Daylight came with a shock for the British as they looked upon the works. Two of the three British officers in charge that day wanted to flank the Americans and take them from the sides but General Howe, still stinging from the spanking the American had given them at Concord, chose a full-on frontal assault. His point was to once again assert British superiority. Trouble was, it was six hours before the tides allowed the attack he planned – six more hours for the Americans to prepare themselves.

General Gage was in the city of Boston watching the Americans with a spyglass and asked one of the Loyalists, Abijah Willard, who was there with him, who the man supervising all that activity was. Willard recognized the man as his own brother in law, William Prescott. Gage asked Willard, "Will he fight?" Willard's response was, "I cannot speak for the men. But Prescott will fight you to the gates of hell."[1] It is William Prescott who is famous for giving the order, "Do not fire until you see the whites of their eyes."

The first American killed was a young man, slain by canon fire just at the crack of dawn. He was immediately buried, after which time, a few hundred men left the American fortifications for home. But the rest of the men did fight.

- **The first British advance was repulsed**
- **As was the second**

Almost 50% of the British soldiers involved were either killed or wounded. When the third advance began, the Americans had just enough ammunition for one final volley. The were commanded to wait until they could see the whites of their eyes, so they could not miss, and then retreat as best they could. Prescott, they say, was one of the last to leave the redoubt crossing swords with the British as he did so.

Technically the Americans lost at Bunker Hill, but one of the British General's later remarked that they could not have afforded a victory like that again. Willard was right – Prescott, and it turned out his men would fight.

A political theorist of the time looked at the odds of the Colonists defeating England and said that while the American were short on ammunition, money and supplies they had this advantage over the British; they were fighting for their liberty. The British were only fighting for an income.

This, I believe, explains why King David's men would fight as they did. The vast majority of them remain unnamed, recorded only in the hallways of eternity. But there were 37 men whose reputations God chose to include in the Bible as

- **An inspiration**
- **An example**
- **A pattern**

for all who would come behind them.

SOME OF THEM WERE INCREDIBLE SOLDIERS

These guys make for great preaching! One guy kills 800 enemies at one time; and he did it with a spear! Another guy fought until his hand wouldn't let go of his sword. Another guy stood in the midst of a bean field and fought off a whole troop of Philistines.

2 Samuel 23:8-12 KJV

These be the names of the mighty men whom David had: The Tachmonite that sat in the seat, chief among the captains; the same was Adino the Eznite: he lift up his spear against eight hundred, whom he slew at one time.

And after him was Eleazar the son of Dodo the Ahohite, one of the three mighty men with David, when they defied the Philistines that were there gathered together to battle, and the men of Israel were gone away:

He arose, and smote the Philistines until his hand was weary, and his hand clave unto the sword: and the LORD wrought a great victory that day; and the people returned after him only to spoil.

And after him was Shammah the son of Agee the Hararite. And the Philistines were gathered together into a troop, where was a piece of ground full of lentils: and the people fled from the Philistines.

But he stood in the midst of the ground, and defended it, and slew the Philistines: and the LORD wrought a great victory.

Abisai killed three hundred enemies by himself.

2 Samuel 23:18 KJV
And Abishai, the brother of Joab, the son of Zeruiah, was chief among three. And he lifted up his spear against three hundred, and slew them, and had the name among three.

Benaiah killed two lion-like men, and then killed an Egyptian one time when he didn't have a weapon. He used his shepherd's staff to disarm the Egyptian and then used the Egyptian's own spear to kill him.

2 Samuel 23:20-21 KJV
And Benaiah the son of Jehoiada, the son of a valiant man, of Kabzeel, who had done many acts, he slew two lionlike men of Moab: he went down also and slew a lion in the midst of a pit in time of snow:
And he slew an Egyptian, a goodly man: and the Egyptian had a spear in his hand; but he went down to him with a staff, and plucked the spear out of the Egyptian's hand, and slew him with his own spear.

No question about it, these are incredible men – heroes on the battlefield!

Everybody loves to hear the stories of heroism in combat.

I just finished reading the account of a famous event that happened in WWII. A formation of B-17 bombers were returning from a mission over Germany when they were assaulted by German fighter planes. One of the B-17 was shot down and Captain Glenn Rojohn moved to position his plane in the slot emptied by the fallen bomber. As he slid into position, he hit another B-17 coming up from below him. The two bombers collided and became stuck together, one right on top of the other. The collision knocked out their engines and of course the thing could not fly like this. But Rojohn knew that if he let go of the controls, the planes would get into a diving spin and would not allow any of the men to parachute out. He and his co-pilot had to prop their legs against the instrument panel in order together to pull hard enough to keep the plane out of a spin long enough for the crew to put on their parachutes and jump. As the plane descended and all of the men who could jump out had, Rojohn ordered his co-pilot to jump. He refused. The two men rode out the fall, miraculously crash landing both planes in such a manner that only one of the men still on board the two planes was killed.

That's a story of almost supernatural heroism. And I thank the Lord for them.

I am also thankful for the heroes in the battle for Christian liberty; people who gave up their own lives to give to us the Bible in the English language.

William Tyndale's dying words were, "Lord, open the eyes of the King of England." Two years later King Henry the VIII authorized the Great Bible to be read in churches. It was almost completely Tyndale's own translation. And just seventy-five years after he was executed, the king now sitting on the throne commissioned a team of men to translate the Bible and give us the King James Version of the Word of God all of us hold.

There were missionaries who gave up their lives so people who had never heard the name of Jesus could be saved.

And there are Baptist preachers who endured beatings and jailings and cruel mockings like you and I could not have believed to ensure that you and I would have the liberty to sit in this room today and hear God's Word preaching loudly and unashamedly.

SOME OF THEM HAD REAL COMPASSION

2 Samuel 23:13-17 KJV

And three of the thirty chief went down, and came to David in the harvest time unto the cave of Adullam: and the troop of the Philistines pitched in the valley of Rephaim.

And David was then in an hold, and the garrison of the Philistines was then in Beth-lehem.

And David longed, and said, Oh that one would give me drink of the water of the well of Beth-lehem, which is by the gate!

And the three mighty men brake through the host of the Philistines, and drew water out of the well of Beth-lehem, that was by the gate, and took it, and brought it to David: nevertheless he would not drink thereof, but poured it out unto the LORD.

And he said, Be it far from me, O LORD, that I should do this: is not this the blood of the men that went in jeopardy of their lives? therefore he would not drink it. These things did these three mighty men.

I think we miss the whole point of this account when we think of King David as more than he was. Remember, the people then did not have a long-standing royal tradition. They had demanded that Samuel give them a king, but it wasn't David. His was a slow ascent to the throne of Israel and his was not a perfect ascent. He had enemies. Even among David's loyal followers there were people he had hurt and people who personally clashed with the King. So, what is recorded in this passage speaks as much or more to the character of these three mighty men – their names are not even recorded – who snuck through enemy lines just to be a blessing to their king.

When you reach out to be a blessing to others, they don't have to be people you think especially deserve your compassion. They don't have to be people you think are perfect and flawless and have always done what you agreed with. How about being a blessing to those God has placed in some position over you – just because it is your character to be a blessing to them and not because they somehow have earned it?

SOME OF THEM WEREN'T SO DIFFERENT FROM YOU AND ME

2 Samuel 23:24-39 KJV

Asahel the brother of Joab was one of the thirty; Elhanan the son of Dodo of Beth-lehem,
Shammah the Harodite, Elika the Harodite,
Helez the Paltite, Ira the son of Ikkesh the Tekoite,
Abiezer the Anethothite, Mebunnai the Hushathite,
Zalmon the Ahohite, Maharai the Netophathite,
Heleb the son of Baanah, a Netophathite, Ittai the son of Ribai out of Gibeah of the children of Benjamin,
Benaiah the Pirathonite, Hiddai of the brooks of Gaash,
Abi-albon the Arbathite, Azmaveth the Barhumite,
Eliahba the Shaalbonite, of the sons of Jashen, Jonathan,
Shammah the Hararite, Ahiam the son of Sharar the Hararite,
Eliphelet the son of Ahasbai, the son of the Maachathite, Eliam the son of Ahithophel the Gilonite,
Hezrai the Carmelite, Paarai the Arbite,
Igal the son of Nathan of Zobah, Bani the Gadite,
Zelek the Ammonite, Naharai the Beerothite, armourbearer to Joab the son of Zeruiah,
Ira an Ithrite, Gareb an Ithrite,
Uriah the Hittite: thirty and seven in all.

The Bible doesn't tell us what these men had done per-se. I know that Uriah the Hittite had enough character that he would not enjoy a night with his wife while others were risking their lives in battle. I know that he obeyed a despicable order to have him moved to an area of combat where he was guaranteed to die. But other than that we don't know anything about these men other than that they were included in David's thirty seven mighty men.

I believe that these men represent what you and I might be in the battle of spiritual liberty, the regular soldier:

- **Whose name may never be recorded for the world to see**
- **Whose deeds of "daring do" will never be entered into the history books of Christianity**

But without whom no victory can ever be won.

Conclusion:

There on Breed's Hill, standing tall and obvious for all to see and recognize, was William Prescott. But there was another man on the hill that day. Dr Joseph Warren was one of Boston's most successful surgeons. He had somehow sensed the night before that he would not survive the upcoming battle and had told his comrades, "These fellows say we won't fight! By Heaven, I hope I shall die up to my knees in blood!"[2] Dr. Warren stayed on Breed's Hill to fight until his death even after he had run out of ammunition, allowing time for the militia to escape.

- **Prescott did fight**
- **Warren did fight but**

So did about 800 other men whose names are not well recorded but whose contribution will never be forgotten.

May I say that in the battle for spiritual liberty we need every one of you to stand your ground.

- **You know I am not speaking about carnal weapons of war today.**
- **You know I am not advocating that you swing you fists or act out in violence.**

I am just saying that the devil would love to get you to:

- **Quit living for God**
- **Quit reading your Bible**
- **Quit bowing your knees in fervent prayer**

Satan would like nothing better than for you to lay down your arms and:

- **Leave your local church**
- **Forsake your faith in Christ**
- **Blend in to the world around you**

Jesus: said "*And ye shall know the truth and the truth shall make you free.*"
John 8:32 KJV

The world, the flesh and the devil would all like to rob you of the truth and bind you into the tyranny of conformity to the world. God says rather, 1 Corinthians 16:13 KJV
Watch ye, stand fast in the faith, quit you like men, be strong.

[1] (Graydon, Alexander; Littell, John Stockton (ed) (1846). Memoirs of His Own Time: With Reminiscences of the Men and Events of the Revolution. Philadelphia: Lindsay & Blakiston. OCLC 1557096.)
[2] http://en.wikipedia.org/wiki/Joseph_Warren

Chapter Ten

MOTHERS IN THE BACKGROUND

Matthew 1:5-6 KJV

And Salmon begat Booz of Rachab; and Booz begat Obed of Ruth; and Obed begat Jesse;
And Jesse begat David the king; and David the king begat Solomon of her that had been the wife of Urias;

Years ago, I read that a famous French general, after meeting George Washington's mother, Mary, said, "It is not surprising that America can produce great men since she can produce great mothers."

Mary Washington was the second wife to her husband, Augustine. Augustine brought in to their marriage two living children. Together they had six additional children. George was the eldest of them. Washington's father, Augustine died when George was only 11 years old. Although Augustine had grown relatively wealthy, almost all of his property passed to the children of his first marriage. Remember, this was in a day when a man was not considered truly "free" unless he owned property. Laws of the land in those days gave the privilege of voting only to land owners. The dictates of the day would have expected Mary, who was only 33 years old, to remarry and care for her and her children's needs through the remarriage, Mary chose not to do that. She managed the small farm that was left to her and her children by herself until George was old enough to take on that responsibility.

Because of the circumstances of his mother's widowhood, George Washington was never able to attend college. Because he was born to his father's second wife, Washington was also considered "second tier" wealth. Yet, through his mother's care and his oldest half brother's guidance, Washington overcame the shortcomings life had given him, to become the father of our nation. Many historians have concluded that, "George Washington's Mother was Essential to His Success"[1]. Washington himself, referred to her as "…my reverend mother by whose maternal hand, early deprived of a father, I was led to manhood."

Memorials to George Washington's mother include:
- **Mary Washington Monument**
- **Mary Washington House**
- **Mary Washington College**
- **Mary Washington Hospital and Healthcare**
- **Mary Washington Museum and Research Center**

When you think about how important a mother is to the character and success of a person, it seems surprising that so few mothers are recorded in the Bible.
- **We do not know the name of Joshua's mother**
- **We do not know the name of the majority of the judges' mothers**
- **We do not know the name of David's mother**
- **We do not know the name of any of the prophets' mothers**
- **We do not know the name of any of the apostles' mothers**

In the four-thousand-year long genealogy of the Lord Jesus Christ, given to us from both His mother and His step-father's side, only four mothers are listed:
- **Thamar**
- **Rahab**
- **Bathsheba**
- **Mary**

These four women, it seems to me, act like four legs that support the chair upon which rests all of the human character of our Saviour.

THAMAR – A PICTURE OF PERSEVERANCE

Genesis 38:24-26 KJV

And it came to pass about three months after, that it was told Judah, saying, Tamar thy daughter in law hath played the harlot; and also, behold, she is with child by whoredom. And Judah said, Bring her forth, and let her be burnt.

When she was brought forth, she sent to her father in law, saying, By the man, whose these are, am I with child: and she said, Discern, I pray thee, whose are these, the signet, and bracelets, and staff.

And Judah acknowledged them, and said, She hath been more righteous than I; because that I gave her not to Shelah my son. And he knew her again no more.

Rather than reading the enter account I will give you the general outline:

Judah has three sons: Er, Onan and Shelah

Er, the oldest, married Tamar

Er is a wicked person. The Bible says God slew him. We live in such a day of grace these days that we hardly think God has the right, to do that! But He does and He did it and I believe, from time to time, He still does. According the customs of the time – in order to preserve the name of a man who dies childless, his widow was to marry her husband's brother and children born of that marriage would carry on the name and memory of the one who had died.

Tamar, according to custom, married Onan,
but because of his disobedience, God slew him too.

There is one more brother, Shelah
But Judah now fears that if Shelah marries Tamar, God might kill him too, so Judah dishonors the memory of his own eldest son by refusing to allow Tamar to marry him.

I am in no way condoning what Tamar did.

When she realized what her father in law was up to, she disguised herself, played the harlot and became pregnant with her father in law's child. When Judah, who was contemplating having Tamar executed for crime of adultery, realized that the child was his very own, he admitted that Tamar had been more righteous than he had been.

While the act of prostitution was immoral then, just as it is now, God's grace overrules the act itself and sets her as a pillar in the genealogy of Christ.

- **She refused to be dismissed from the family of Judah**
- **She refused to be removed from the line that would lead to Christ**
- **She persevered, as it were, in her faith and was recognized for it.**

She reminds me of the woman of Canaan whose daughter was "vexed with a devil". It looked like the Lord was putting her off. She was begging Him for help, but He answered not a word. The disciples obvious rebuffed her too as they asked Jesus to send her away. Once more she begs the Lord and this time He responds, *"It is not meet to take the children's bread, and cast it to dogs."* You would think that would be enough to discourage her but she comes back to Him with, *"Truth, Lord: yet the dogs eat of the crumbs which fall from their master's table."*[2] She just would not be excluded from the blessings of the Lord.

RAHAB – A PICTURE OF REPENTANCE

Joshua 2:9-13 KJV

And she said unto the men, I know that the LORD hath given you the land, and that your terror is fallen upon us, and that all the inhabitants of the land faint because of you.

For we have heard how the LORD dried up the water of the Red sea for you, when ye came out of Egypt; and what ye did unto the two kings of

the Amorites, that were on the other side Jordan, Sihon and Og, whom ye utterly destroyed.
And as soon as we had heard these things, our hearts did melt, neither did there remain any more courage in any man, because of you: for the LORD your God, he is God in heaven above, and in earth beneath.
Now therefore, I pray you, swear unto me by the LORD, since I have shewed you kindness, that ye will also shew kindness unto my father's house, and give me a true token:
And that ye will save alive my father, and my mother, and my brethren, and my sisters, and all that they have, and deliver our lives from death.

Rahab is another harlot mentioned in the genealogy of Jesus. She, like the woman whose daughter was vexed with a devil, was a Canaanite and she, along with her entire city of Jericho, was about to experience the judgment of God at the hands of Joshua and the Israelites. All of the Canaanites were afraid of the Jews; Rahab acknowledged that. But only she, and those in her family that she was able to convince to enter into her house, turned from their sin instead of kicking against God.

Jericho is a type of the condition of the world. It is condemned already, facing the judgment of almighty God. The citizens are a type of the majority of the population of this world. They do not relish the idea of God's judgment. They do not want to go to hell.

- **But they refuse to get right with God to avoid it**
- **Some get downright belligerent and fight God over it**

Rahab and her family serve as a type of those who get saved out of this world.

She was still there in Jericho, she did her best to get people to come under her roof and be saved and when the judgment came, she and those with her were added to the people of God.

It has always been the minority of people who
*** Repent of their sins**

*** Trust the Lord Jesus Christ**
*** Become the people of God**

But, just as Rahab made the right choice, so does anyone who becomes a true Christian.

BATHSHEBA – A PICTURE OF CONTENTEDNESS

2 Samuel 12:15-25 KJV

And Nathan departed unto his house. And the LORD struck the child that Uriah's wife bare unto David, and it was very sick.

David therefore besought God for the child; and David fasted, and went in, and lay all night upon the earth.

And the elders of his house arose, and went to him, to raise him up from the earth: but he would not, neither did he eat bread with them.

And it came to pass on the seventh day, that the child died. And the servants of David feared to tell him that the child was dead: for they said, Behold, while the child was yet alive, we spake unto him, and he would not hearken unto our voice: how will he then vex himself, if we tell him that the child is dead?

But when David saw that his servants whispered, David perceived that the child was dead: therefore David said unto his servants, Is the child dead? And they said, He is dead.

Then David arose from the earth, and washed, and anointed himself, and changed his apparel, and came into the house of the LORD, and worshipped: then he came to his own house; and when he required, they set bread before him, and he did eat.

Then said his servants unto him, What thing is this that thou hast done? thou didst fast and weep for the child, while it was alive; but when the child was dead, thou didst rise and eat bread.

And he said, While the child was yet alive, I fasted and wept: for I said, Who can tell whether GOD will be gracious to me, that the child may live?

But now he is dead, wherefore should I fast? can I bring him back again? I shall go to him, but he shall not return to me.

And David comforted Bathsheba his wife, and went in unto her, and lay with her: and she bare a son, and he called his name Solomon: and the LORD loved him.

From a worldly point of view Bathsheba would have had every reason to have lived out the remainder of her life a bitter, angry person.

She had been abused by the King.
In those days she would have had no say and no means to repulse the advances of her king. Some say she should not have been bathing where she was. The Bible doesn't say that. What we learn in the Bible is that David had no business being home when she was bathing.
* **He saw her**
* **He called her**
* **He was the one rebuked for what they did**

David had her husband killed in battle.
Uriah did not die, as they say, from the "fortunes of war" but was murdered at the hands of King David just as if David had stabbed him in the stomach like Joab killed Abner.

The baby that had been conceived in their sin got ill and died.
For some women, this would have been enough to "take them over the edge". Not Bathsheba. Once the child had died the Bible says, David, the one who started this whole spiral downward, "comforted Bathsheba, his wife." The Bible text began with her being described as "Uriah's wife" vs 15 but ends describing her as David's wife.

In other words, she moved on. She didn't let hardships and heartbreaks deprive her of
- **Hope**
- **Joy**
- **Reason to look ahead**

She was comforted by David.
- **She and David conceived at least one more baby and**

- **She became the mother of the next King in Israel**

Everyone of us face hardships and heartaches of one form or another. Granted, some seem to go through things that appear more difficult than other go through. But all of us have the same choice when it comes to those hardships and heartaches; will they make us bitter or will we break through them and go forward in
- **hopefulness,**
- **contendedness and**
- **joy?**

MARY – A PICTURE OF GODLINESS

Luke 1:26-31 KJV
And in the sixth month the angel Gabriel was sent from God unto a city of Galilee, named Nazareth,
To a virgin espoused to a man whose name was Joseph, of the house of David; and the virgin's name was Mary.
And the angel came in unto her, and said, Hail, thou that art highly favoured, the Lord is with thee: blessed art thou among women.
And when she saw him, she was troubled at his saying, and cast in her mind what manner of salutation this should be.
And the angel said unto her, Fear not, Mary: for thou hast found favour with God.
And, behold, thou shalt conceive in thy womb, and bring forth a son, and shalt call his name JESUS.

We are told twice in this passage that Mary was a virgin and twice that she was favored of the Lord.

The term virgin refers to her purity.
I can promise you that Mary was not sinless. I am able to say that one two counts:
First, the Bible says "…*all have sinned, and come short of the glory of God.*"
All would include Mary.

Second Mary herself admitted she needed a Saviour
Luke 1:46-47 KJV
And Mary said, My soul doth magnify the Lord,
And my spirit hath rejoiced in God my Saviour.
She is not sinless, but neither is she promiscuous.

Here is how that relates to you and me;
- **All of us are sinners – we can't help that**
- **But none of us have to live in sin**

We can choose to turn from sin and refuse to let it have dominion in our lives.

The term favor refers to God's grace
Mary, I am sure, was not the only virgin in Israel that year. But she is the one that God chose to be the mother of our Saviour.

For every one of us there is something we can do and something only God can do for us. Mary teaches us to do the thing we can do and rest in the Lord to do what we can't. That, I would suggest, is the definition of true godliness.

Conclusion
Four thousand years of family leading from Adam to Jesus Christ and the Bible only gives us the names of four of the mothers who delivered this family. I think they are singled out not because the others are unimportant but because these four illustrate qualities of value for each of us.

- **Thamar represents perseverance**
- **Rahab represents repentance**
- **Bathsheba represents contentedness**
- **Mary represents godliness**

[1] http://www.ourherald.com/news/2008-07-03/Front_Page/f06.html, accessed 5-7-2015

Then Jesus went thence, and departed into the coasts of Tyre and Sidon.

And, behold, a woman of Canaan came out of the same coasts, and cried unto him, saying, Have mercy on me, O Lord, thou Son of David; my daughter is grievously vexed with a devil.

But he answered her not a word. And his disciples came and besought him, saying, Send her away; for she crieth after us.

But he answered and said, I am not sent but unto the lost sheep of the house of Israel.

Then came she and worshipped him, saying, Lord, help me.

But he answered and said, It is not meet to take the children's bread, and to cast it to dogs.

And she said, Truth, Lord: yet the dogs eat of the crumbs which fall from their masters' table.

Then Jesus answered and said unto her, O woman, great is thy faith: be it unto thee even as thou wilt. And her daughter was made whole from that very hour.

Chapter Eleven

PLAY THE MEN

2 Samuel 10:9-12 KJV

When Joab saw that the front of the battle was against him before and behind, he chose of all the choice men of Israel, and put them in array against the Syrians:

And the rest of the people he delivered into the hand of Abishai his brother, that he might put them in array against the children of Ammon.

And he said, If the Syrians be too strong for me, then thou shalt help me: but if the children of Ammon be too strong for thee, then I will come and help thee.

Be of good courage, and let us play the men for our people, and for the cities of our God: and the LORD do that which seemeth him good.

August of 1777, an American Militia General by the name of Nicolas Herkimer received word that the British, under General Johnny Burgoyne, were making their way down from Canada and that a contingent of them had laid siege to the nearby American Fort Stanwix.[1]

Herkimer mustered about 800 local militiamen, mostly farmers, and set out to give aide to the garrison stationed at the Fort. When he got near Herkimer hesitated. Some of his men speculated

- **That he was afraid**
- **That he had loyalist sympathies**
- **That he did not want to fight these British because his own brother was among them**

It turned out that Herkimer's hesitations were well founded as, when they advanced, they walked straight into an ambush. The British attack Herkimer with about 500 British Regulars and Hessian mercenaries, and an additional force of Mohawk Indians numbering as many as 500. In the early moments of the surprise attack Colonel Ebenezer Cox was killed and General Herkimer was badly wounded in his leg. The initial shock of the attack sent Herkimer's militia into a panic. His men were militia – untested and not very skilled. They say it took each of them upwards of 15 minutes to load his gun after he fired.

Herkimer, though wounded, ordered his aides to lean him up against a tree. There he lit his pipe and calmly began issuing orders to his troops. His calm in the face of the enemy gave courage to his troops. They kept fighting until a storm arose and forced the British to cease-fire for an hour. Herkimer used that hour to reform his lines and to issue a new command – the men were to fight in pairs, one firing while the other was reloading so that none of them were caught unarmed when an Indian warrior raced toward them with a tomahawk.

When the battle was over the British were the ones who were forced from the field, but the Americans had lost almost 500 of the 800 men killed, wounded or taken prisoner. "Though traditionally seen as a clear American defeat, the Battle of Oriskany marked a turning point in St. Leger's campaign in western New York. Angered by the losses taken at Oriskany, his Native American allies became increasingly disgruntled as they had not anticipated in taking part in large, pitched battles."[2] Today New York has both a town and a county named after Herkimer.

The Battle of Oriskany reminded me of the battle that took place between Israel's men and the Ammonites in 2 Samuel 10.

THE ACTION BEGAN BECAUSE OF A CRITICAL PERSONALITY
2 Samuel 10:1-7 KJV

And it came to pass after this, that the king of the children of Ammon died, and Hanun his son reigned in his stead.

Then said David, I will shew kindness unto Hanun the son of Nahash, as his father shewed kindness unto me. And David sent to comfort him by the hand of his servants for his father. And David's servants came into the land of the children of Ammon.

And the princes of the children of Ammon said unto Hanun their lord, Thinkest thou that David doth honour thy father, that he hath sent comforters unto thee? hath not David rather sent his servants unto thee, to search the city, and to spy it out, and to overthrow it?

Wherefore Hanun took David's servants, and shaved off the one half of their beards, and cut off their garments in the middle, even to their buttocks, and sent them away.

When they told it unto David, he sent to meet them, because the men were greatly ashamed: and the king said, Tarry at Jericho until your beards be grown, and then return.

And when the children of Ammon saw that they stank before David, the children of Ammon sent and hired the Syrians of Bethrehob, and the Syrians of Zoba, twenty thousand footmen, and of king Maacah a thousand men, and of Ish-tob twelve thousand men.

And when David heard of it, he sent Joab, and all the host of the mighty men.

All of the bloodshed, all of the death, all of the:
- **Hard feelings**
- **Anger**
- **Pain**

that happens in this chapter is because someone chose to speak unkindly about another person. They were wrong – but that did not matter. The damage they did by saying negative things about King David was undoable.

Don't be this person. Learn how to speak kindly about others or learn not to speak at all!

James 3:3-10 KJV
Behold, we put bits in the horses' mouths, that they may obey us; and we turn about their whole body.

Behold also the ships, which though they be so great, and are driven of fierce winds, yet are they turned about with a very small helm, whithersoever the governor listeth.

Even so the tongue is a little member, and boasteth great things. Behold, how great a matter a little fire kindleth!

And the tongue is a fire, a world of iniquity: so is the tongue among our members, that it defileth the whole body, and setteth on fire the course of nature; and it is set on fire of hell.

For every kind of beasts, and of birds, and of serpents, and of things in the sea, is tamed, and hath been tamed of mankind:

But the tongue can no man tame; it is an unruly evil, full of deadly poison.

Therewith bless we God, even the Father; and therewith curse we men, which are made after the similitude of God.

Out of the same mouth proceedeth blessing and cursing. My brethren, these things ought not so to be.

Maybe the most powerful part of this passage is the very last phrase, "My brethren, these things ought not so to be." And yet they are. I know people:

- **Who have quit drinking, smoking, and gambling**
- **Who have repented of immorality and promiscuity**
- **Who have recovered from laziness and greed**

But I know very few who will even admit that they have a problem with their tongue.

The damage that is caused by the tongue!

By 1778 the French had been convinced to join with American Colonialists to help them defeat the British and gain independence. The first cooperative campaign between the French and American forces against Britain was to be in Rhode Island. In charge of the French was their Admiral d'Estaing. The Americans were led by General John Sullivan, a man who had been elected to the position. Later John Adams would say of Sullivan something to the effect of, "It would have been best if the first British canon fired had taken off his head."

The French and Americans agreed to begin their campaign on a particular day, but Sullivan got impatient and began too early. The French, who still regarded the Americans and unskilled in warfare, too offense and did not reinforce the Americans. The Americans lost, sending Sullivan into a tirade, publicly denouncing the French of desertion and saying that the French Admiral had dishonored his country. Infuriated, the French sailed away, leaving America to fight on without their help.

The French navy did not return until 1781.

One man with an unruly tongue ruined the relationship between the Americans and the French and probably cost the lives of thousands more Americans who, had the war ended two or three years earlier, would have survived.

THE ENEMY HIRED OTHERS TO HELP HIM

2 Samuel 10:6 KJV
And when the children of Ammon saw that they stank before David, the children of Ammon sent and hired the Syrians of Bethrehob, and the Syrians of Zoba, twenty thousand footmen, and of king Maacah a thousand men, and of Ish-tob twelve thousand men.

Very seldom will you find this world friendly to your cause as a Christian. Less seldom will you find that, when they attack, they do so in gracious ways.

David sent Joab and the armies to do what was their job to do, but it wasn't going to be easy.
2 Samuel 10:8-9 KJV

And the children of Ammon came out, and put the battle in array at the entering in of the gate: and the Syrians of Zoba, and of Rehob, and Ish-tob, and Maacah, were by themselves in the field.
When Joab saw that the front of the battle was against him before and behind,…

I am very thankful I get to live in the United States of America. I love our country and love the freedoms we have enjoyed. But the fact is, we are going down hill very fast. We are a nation filled with people who believe they are:
- **Entitled to a living,**
- **Entitled to government handouts**
- **Entitled to live as they please without consequences**

That same spirit has infiltrated our churches so that the average Christian turns tail and runs if the going gets hard in the least.
- **Where are the Christians when it comes time to go out visiting?**
- **Where are the Christians when the church calls for a work day?**
- **Where are the Christians when there is a SS class to fill?**
- **Where are the Christians who will work the bus routes or pray for the destitute or help out a fallen soul?**

I don't want to accuse anyone because I can't know the hearts of men; but I know that when the battle seems against them, some of them are out looking for an easier way.

JOAB CALMLY CREATED A WINNING STRATEGY

2 Samuel 10:9-12 KJV
When Joab saw that the front of the battle was against him before and behind, he chose of all the choice men of Israel, and put them in array against the Syrians:

I was at Tacoma General Hospital the other night. I was alone in the elevator where I saw a sign that struck me funny. It said, "In case the elevator stops, KEEP CALM…." followed by instructions. The words KEEP CALM were capitalized. The reason I thought it was funny is because I know me. If I was not able to remain calm, none of the rest of the instructions would have made any difference to me. I couldn't make most of them out as it was. It was a pretty long list – none of them were capitalized, only those two words. KEEP CALM.

It is amazing what a person can do if they just remain calm.

The British had a Scottish officer by the name of Captain Patrick Ferguson. Ferguson was considered to be the best marksman in the British army and commanded a detachment of sharpshooters. Ferguson had personally designed an early repeating rifle that was capable of firing seven aimed rounds per minute. (Remember, some of the Colonial Militia took 15 minutes to reload.) Days before the Battle of Brandywine, Ferguson and his marksman, each armed with his new repeating rifle, was patrolling the area in preparation for the expected battle. He and his men came across two American officers. He ordered his men to sneak up to them and kill them. But then, according to accounts given later, he was overwhelmed with disgust and the prospect of shooting these two men who were so calmly conducting themselves. When he yelled out to them, he said Washington looked his way, turned his horse and casually rode off of the field.

At the Battle of Cowpens, Daniel Morgan won what has been called the second most important victory of the American Revolution. He did it by allowing his men to simply do what they were capable of doing and no more. First in line of combat were his sharpshooters. Their job was to pick off as many officers as they could right away. Next were his militiamen. The militias were volunteers. They were just local guys with a gun, and they were notorious for running from the British, especially when they saw their bayonets. Finally, were his regulars. These were his disciplined troops.

The night before the battle, Morgan rode into the camp of the militia and asked them to fire just two shots then to disperse. He said that if they would give him just those two rounds, they could return home and count themselves heroes.

The next day they fired their two rounds and took off running for home just like Morgan told them they could do. The British, figuring they had them beat, fixed bayonets and pursued after them and ran smack into the American regulars. The British were decimated. Over half their men were lost. More than 800 of them just "laid down" on the field and were captured. Historians say that it was "combat shock" a combination of hunger exhaustion and fright – they lost their will to fight.

The second greatest victory in the Revolutionary war was won all because the American stayed calm and did what was asked of them.

Joab enters into this battle arena and realizes this thing could turn out very badly. But he didn't panic. He divided his men between himself and his brother, Abishai and gave them a plan. Abishai and his men would face the Syrians. He and his men would face the Ammonites

He assured them, if one side became overwhelmed, the other side would come and help them. He urged them:
- **Be of good courage**
- **Play the men**

And the rest of it will be in God's hands.

And that is all that God asks of you. Just:
- **Be in your place**
- **Help each other when there is a need**
- **Don't say negative or damaging things**

Then trust God to do what is right.

[1] Now Rome, New York
[2]http://militaryhistory.about.com/od/AmRev1777/p/American-Revolution-Battle-Of-Oriskany.htm, accessed 5-15-15

Chapter Twelve

JUST ONE LIFE

Hebrews 9:24-28 KJV

For Christ is not entered into the holy places made with hands, which are the figures of the true; but into heaven itself, now to appear in the presence of God for us:
Nor yet that he should offer himself often, as the high priest entereth into the holy place every year with blood of others;
For then must he often have suffered since the foundation of the world: but now once in the end of the world hath he appeared to put away sin by the sacrifice of himself.
And as it is appointed unto men once to die, but after this the judgment:
So Christ was once offered to bear the sins of many; and unto them that look for him shall he appear the second time without sin unto salvation.

Nathan Hale was just twenty-one years old when the British caught him in New York and arrested him as a spy. Hale was a graduate of Yale University and, by the time of the War for Independence, was already a seasoned schoolteacher. By all accounts he was a quiet, peaceable young man, but he was also patriotic and sacrificial.

He was nineteen years old when, in 1774, joined his local militia unit. After the conflict at Lexington and Concord, Nathan Hale resigned his position as a teacher in New London, Connecticut, and joined the official Continental Army. Hale was chosen to be a part of a special unit that was called "Norton's Rangers" some people say that we would call them in today's term "Special Forces."

In September of 1776, George Washington, desperate to gain intelligence of the British activities assigned Nolton the task of coming up with a plan to get that information. Hale volunteered to infiltrate the city of New York disguised as a Dutch schoolteacher. He was turned by some suspicious loyalists in New York and hanged to death September 22, 1776.

Executions in those days were nothing like they would be today. He was hanged very shortly after his sentence and with very few witnesses except for British military personnel. However, one of the British officers present did briefly record the event in his personal journal and one of Nathan Hale's Yale classmates, and a personal friend, William Hull, was able under a flag of truce, to interview the officer in charge the next day. It was Hull that reported that among Hale's last words was the famous line, "I regret that I have but one life to lose for my country."

As famous as the statement is, the sacrifice of Nathan Hale almost became a forgotten event in the history of the United States. Hundreds of soldiers lost their lives that September. Hale was only one of them. George Washington never mentioned the name of Nathan Hale in any of his written documents. Neither did any of the other founders of our country. It wasn't until the early 1900's that the story of Nathan Hale began to take on the fame it has today.

For that reason Nathan Hale serves as a representative for all of those forgotten men who lost their lives to purchase the liberty we enjoy today. I want to use his story as a springboard to point out those who gave their lives, not for the liberty of a country, but for the souls of men and women. The battle for spiritual liberty traces all the way back to the death of Abel at the hands of his brother, Cain. Millions of people have died to:

- **Preserve**
- **Protect**
- **Propagate**

our faith.

It would be impossible to identify them all, let alone bring a message that incorporates them all. I want instead to acknowledge the sacrifice of those original disciples of the Lord Jesus Christ.

SOME DIED VERY EARLY

Of the original followers, the first to give his life for the faith was

A. A deacon named Stephen

Acts 7:55-59 KJV

But he, being full of the Holy Ghost, looked up stedfastly into heaven, and saw the glory of God, and Jesus standing on the right hand of God,
And said, Behold, I see the heavens opened, and the Son of man standing on the right hand of God.
Then they cried out with a loud voice, and stopped their ears, and ran upon him with one accord,
And cast him out of the city, and stoned him: and the witnesses laid down their clothes at a young man's feet, whose name was Saul.
And they stoned Stephen, calling upon God, and saying, Lord Jesus, receive my spirit.

Stephen might remind me the most of all of the men I will consider today of Nathan Hale.

- **He wasn't one of the 12 apostles**
- **He wasn't included in any of the great miracles in the gospels**

He was an ordinary man.

- **But he was full of faith and the Holy Ghost**

And others noticed it. When the twelve apostles asked for the members of the church to find some men who were, "of honest report, full of the Holy Ghost and wisdom" Stephen was one of the seven men they recommended.

I wonder, would anyone recognize your walk with God and recommend you to help a preacher out?

It was only ordinary men who were destined to pay the price for their faith. Very early on in Christian history, the Bible records the execution of,

B. Apostle James

Acts 12:1-2 KJV

Now about that time Herod the king stretched forth his hands to vex certain of the church.

And he killed James the brother of John with the sword.

There is another man in the Bible with the same name – the writer of the Book of James and the half brother of Jesus Christ. The James of Acts 12 is a different man. James was the brother of the Apostle John. The two of them were the sons of Zebedee and among the very first to leave their old lives to follow Jesus. So close was this man to the Lord Jesus Christ that we often refer to him and his brother John and Peter as "Christ's inner circle."

These three men went places with Jesus no one else ever did. In my mind this begs the question, "How far will you go with Jesus Christ?"

Of those who gave their lives so we might have faith in Christ,

MOST DIED VIOLENTLY

I suppose it is a blessing that the Bible doesn't give the record of the execution and deaths of all of the Apostles. Truth is, we have the record of just two deaths: Stephen and James.

The concept of persecution – even to death is carried throughout the New Testament. Hebrews 12:4 KJV

Ye have not yet resisted unto blood, striving against sin.

Hebrews 11:13 KJV
These all died in faith, not having received the promises, but having seen them afar off, and were persuaded of them, and embraced them, and confessed that they were strangers and pilgrims on the earth.

There are hints of the impending death of Paul and of Peter and the Apostle John was exiled on the Isle of Patmos for the testimony of Christ. But I for one am glad that the New Testament doesn't go in to the gruesome details of the gory deaths of the apostles.

What we know about the other apostles besides Paul and Peter is sketchy at best. There are no real historical records or even eye witness testimonials. What exists is merely tradition; stories handed down from one person to the next.
* **Some of them probably have some truth in them**
* **Some of them are completely fictional**

What we can be assured of is that these men
* **Took the Gospel around the world**
* **Gave their lives that the world may know Jesus Christ**

A. Some of them were killed by crucifixion
Government authority

B. Some of them were killed by angry mobs
Murdered for nothing more than preaching that Jesus Christ forgives the sins of those who trust Him.

C. One of them lived to be nearly100 years old
And, though persecuted for his faith, never backed down on his message that Jesus Christ:
* **Lived a sinless life**
* **Died a sacrificial death**
* **Arose a victor of the grave**

The Bible says, Ephesians 2:19-20 KJV
Now therefore ye are no more strangers and foreigners, but fellowcitizens with the saints, and of the household of God;
And are built upon the foundation of the apostles and prophets, Jesus Christ himself being the chief corner stone;

I wonder, are you building on that foundation? If the gospel were left to you alone – would the next generation get to know the same message you heard concerning Jesus Christ?

ONE DIED FOR ALL

Hebrews 9:27-28 KJV
And as it is appointed unto men once to die, but after this the judgment:
So Christ was once offered to bear the sins of many; and unto them that look for him shall he appear the second time without sin unto salvation.

Nathan Hale had but one life he could lose for his country.
- **His service was selfless**
- **His sacrifice was valiant**

But then, as he knew only too well, there was nothing more he could give.

Not so with Jesus Christ. He did die but once – but in His case, once was enough.
- **Because his life was perfect**
- **Because His sacrifice was divine**
- **Because He then rose again**

The death, the burial and the resurrection of Jesus Christ has never ceased to give.

Hebrews 7:25 KJV
Wherefore he is able also to save them to the uttermost that come unto God by him, seeing he ever liveth to make intercession for them.

He gave just one life, and that one life is able to save

* **Anyone**
* **Anywhere**
* **Any time**

So that the promise of God's Word is,
Romans 10:13 KJV
For whosoever shall call upon the name of the Lord shall be saved.

Of those early followers of Jesus Christ,

ONE DIED FAITHLESSLY

Matthew 27:3-5 KJV
Then Judas, which had betrayed him, when he saw that he was condemned, repented himself, and brought again the thirty pieces of silver to the chief priests and elders,
Saying, I have sinned in that I have betrayed the innocent blood. And they said, What is that to us? see thou to that.
And he cast down the pieces of silver in the temple, and departed, and went and hanged himself.

The true shame of Judas Iscariot is not that he betrayed Christ. Peter denied the Lord three times but then went on to be mightily used of the Lord. It isn't even that he killed himself, although that is a huge tragedy. The heartbreak of the story of Judas Iscariot is that he did not trust Christ. If he had, he, like Peter, could have risen above his treacherous act and been once again blessed of God. His sin was that, though he had followed Christ and pretended to be a believer in Christ – he had not trusted Christ.

His story reminds us all that:

* **Being religious**
* **Attending services**
* **Calling ourselves Christian**

isn't enough.

How many are those who seem to be great believers but, in the end, turn out to be false professors?

Chapter Thirteen

A NEW CREATURE

1 Kings 9:26-27 KJV

And king Solomon made a navy of ships in Ezion-geber, which is beside Eloth, on the shore of the Red sea, in the land of Edom.
And Hiram sent in the navy his servants, shipmen that had knowledge of the sea, with the servants of Solomon.

Did you know that many of Revolutionary War "patriots" were not actually from this continent? When settlers began arriving here in the early 1600's, they came really for a new beginning.

- **For some it was freedom to worship God according to the dictates of their own conscience**
- **For some it was for the opportunity to possess land and the liberty to create wealth through it**
- **For some it was a chance to become free from the problems they faced in their mother country**

One hundred fifty years later America was on the verge of a revolution from England, but Europeans, stilled flocked to this place for a chance at a new life. Some of them were only here for months before they were neck deep in Revolutionary sentiment. Some of them came just for the Revolution. I will use the stories of three of those men today to illustrate the opportunities that belong to you and me as Christians.

2 Corinthians 5:17 KJV

Therefore if any man be in Christ, he is a new creature: old things are passed away; behold, all things are become new.

- **No matter what our past has held**
- **No matter where we have come from**
- **No matter what we once believed**
- **No matter what we may have done**

When a person becomes a Christian, he becomes a citizen of a new country and a new creature through Jesus Christ.

- **Old things pass away**
- **All things become new**

I'll begin with the story of Thomas Paine and use him to describe,

A NEW BEGINNING

A. Thomas Paine was born in England where he lived until the age of 38.

Frankly he had not done well.

- **He had failed in business (twice)**
- **He had been fired as a tax collector (twice)**
- **He was divorced from his wife**

The only thing that he really had going for him was:

- **His political sentiments**
- **An ability to write**
- **An introduction to Benjamin Franklin**

Franklin suggested that he might do better in the colonies and sponsored his move. (Franklin saw in him a fiery advocate for American Independence.) Paine came to America nearly penniless. But he arrived at a fortuitous moment in time for a man with his particular talents.

- **He was anti-England**
- **He was a fiery personality**
- **He was a passionate writer**

It did not take him long at all to see that Americans all over the place were talking the same sorts of things he had been thinking. He published Common Sense in January of 1776, it was an immediate success and sold almost as many copies as was being sold of the Bible at the period. Common Sense virtually launched America into a Revolutionary War mindset. Not much later Paine wrote The American Crisis, which

Washington had read aloud to his soldiers just previous to crossing the Delaware and attacking the Hessians at Trenton.

B. I see Zacchaeus as a sort of New Testament counterpart to Thomas Paine.
Luke 19:1-10 KJV
And Jesus entered and passed through Jericho.
And, behold, there was a man named Zacchaeus, which was the chief among the publicans, and he was rich.
And he sought to see Jesus who he was; and could not for the press, because he was little of stature.
And he ran before, and climbed up into a sycomore tree to see him: for he was to pass that way.
And when Jesus came to the place, he looked up, and saw him, and said unto him, Zacchaeus, make haste, and come down; for to day I must abide at thy house.
And he made haste, and came down, and received him joyfully.
And when they saw it, they all murmured, saying, That he was gone to be guest with a man that is a sinner.
And Zacchaeus stood, and said unto the Lord; Behold, Lord, the half of my goods I give to the poor; and if I have taken any thing from any man by false accusation, I restore him fourfold.
And Jesus said unto him, This day is salvation come to this house, forsomuch as he also is a son of Abraham.
For the Son of man is come to seek and to save that which was lost.

Zacchaeus was not well loved and not well mannered.
- **He made his living as a tax collector for the Romans**
- **He had extorted who knows how much from his brethren in Israel**

but when he met Jesus Christ – he received a whole new beginning for his life.

C. Christ offers every one of us that same brand new beginning
Because of the death, burial and resurrection, "whosoever will" may call on the name of the Lord and
- **Be forgiven of their sins**

- **Be born again into the family of God**
- **Be made a new creature**

There is a new beginning.

Let me tell you the story of John Paul Jones and use him to describe,

A NEW NAME

A. I was fascinated to learn that John Paul Jones, the famous naval hero of the Revolutionary war, was not his name.

Jones was born in Scotland and was originally named just John Paul.

- **He began his career as a sailor at the age of 12**
- **He had advanced, through his years at sea, to the position of a merchant captain**

John Paul was a notoriously strict disciplinarian onboard the ships he captained. One of his crewmen died of a flogging he received. John Paul spent time in prison for the man's death but was later released on bail. He got a position as the captain of another ship, but in a dispute over wages, killed a man on that ship with a sword. Not willing to risk trial for that death, John Paul changed his name to the now famous John Paul Jones and fled to Virginia.

Very shortly after arriving in the colonies, John Paul Jones travelled to Philadelphia and offered himself for service in the battle for independence. Because of his experience as a ship's captain he was given a commission as an officer in the newly formed Continental Navy.

Jones was a fairly successful captain in his naval career but his fame propelled when he was given command of the French made, Bonhomme Richard. While in command of that ship, he came against a much more powerfully gunned British ship called HMS Serapis. As the battle progressed, Jones brought his ship alongside the Serapis, lashed himself to it and fought so closely together that witnesses said you could hear the captains of the two ships yelling at each other. Jones' ship was getting pummeled by the Serapis but he refused to give up. At some point in the battle he was heard to say, "I have not yet begun to fight." The captain of the Serapis, Richard Pearson, decided that Jones was crazy and would sink both ships before he surrendered. Pearson surrendered instead.

For Jones, America offered a new start and a new name.

B. Christ gives to each person who is born again his own brand new name

Revelation 2:17 KJV

He that hath an ear, let him hear what the Spirit saith unto the churches; To him that overcometh will I give to eat of the hidden manna, and will give him a white stone, and in the stone a new name written, which no man knoweth saving he that receiveth it.

Revelation 3:12 KJV

Him that overcometh will I make a pillar in the temple of my God, and he shall go no more out: and I will write upon him the name of my God, and the name of the city of my God, which is new Jerusalem, which cometh down out of heaven from my God: and I will write upon him my new name.

I maybe know better than most what a new name can mean in a person's life because my last name is not the one I was born with. I have nothing critical to say about my natural father or my family on his side. But for me that name is associated with a whole lot of grief and tears. Frankly, I hid under the alias of

McKenzie until after I met Anita. When we started talking about marriage she told me that she would accept either name as her own, but she would not accept an alias. She required me to pick one name or the other and claim it legally and openly. Just before our wedding, the courts allowed me to legally change my name to McKenzie.

For me, the very best days of my life have all happened under that new name.

Notice three things the Lord gives us with our new name:
1. He gives us hidden manna
That's the Word of God, "*Man shall not live by bread alone, but by every word that proceedeth out of the mouth of God.*"

It's hidden manna because only those who are saved and have the new name can eat and enjoy it.

2. He gives us a white stone
And writes our new name on it.
- **White speaks of holiness**
- **Stone speak of permanence**

When we get saved God makes us righteous that cannot be taken away from us.

3. He gives us to be a pillar in His temple
As a Christian:
- **I have a place in God's house**
- **I have a function in God's house**

I am not just a flower that acts as an ornament for a bit and then shrivels away. I am a piece of the structure of God's house. If you remove me, you damage the whole thing.

I have been a member of a local church long enough to know that there is no such thing as an expendable member in the church. Every member who leaves,

- **No matter who they are**
- **No matter why they leave**

Hurts the church –and it never truly recovers.

My last story concerns the Marquis de Lafayette whom I will use to describe,

A NEW VISION

A. Lafayette was born an Aristocrat, but was no spoiled brat

He was trained in military tactics and commissioned as an officer at age 13. At age 19 Lafayette became enchanted with the American cause, purchased a ship and sailed for America. Washington made him a Major General. He was wounded at Brandywine and served with distinction alongside General Washington throughout the war.[1]

After the war Lafayette went back home to fight (not so successfully) for the same ideals he had seen in America. He lived his entire life pursuing those ideals for his own country, even spending many years exiled and in prison for those convictions. He had grown up in wealth and aristocracy but had seen the pitiful condition of those who were not born into wealth.

For Lafayette, America offered a vision of a new sort of life where free men, created equally, served one another for a greater good.

B. Christianity offers the believer a new purpose for his own life

No longer do we wake up to, "Get all we can and can all we get." Christians possess all of heaven. Why would we ever scrap to collect the trinkets of the world?

- **We have a vision of souls being saved**
- **We have a vision of churches being supported**
- **We have a vision united among brethren**

And though we don't always see our vision completely fulfilled, it is still the thing we live and fight for because

- **We also have a vision of Jesus Christ coming again**

Conclusion
2 Corinthians 5:17 KJV
Therefore if any man be in Christ, he is a new creature: old things are passed away; behold, all things are become new.

All things are become new
- **A new beginning**
- **A new name**
- **A new vision**

[1] With a short intermission to return to France and lobby for his country's assistance for the American cause.

Chapter Fourteen

A HOUSE DIVIDED

1 Kings 11:43 KJV

And Solomon slept with his fathers, and was buried in the city of David his father: and Rehoboam his son reigned in his stead.

1 Kings 12:1-17 KJV

And Rehoboam went to Shechem: for all Israel were come to Shechem to make him king.

And it came to pass, when Jeroboam the son of Nebat, who was yet in Egypt, heard of it, (for he was fled from the presence of king Solomon, and Jeroboam dwelt in Egypt;)

That they sent and called him. And Jeroboam and all the congregation of Israel came, and spake unto Rehoboam, saying,

Thy father made our yoke grievous: now therefore make thou the grievous service of thy father, and his heavy yoke which he put upon us, lighter, and we will serve thee.

And he said unto them, Depart yet for three days, then come again to me. And the people departed.

And king Rehoboam consulted with the old men, that stood before Solomon his father while he yet lived, and said, How do ye advise that I may answer this people?

And they spake unto him, saying, If thou wilt be a servant unto this people this day, and wilt serve them, and answer them, and speak good words to them, then they will be thy servants for ever.

But he forsook the counsel of the old men, which they had given him, and consulted with the young men that were grown up with him, and which stood before him:

And he said unto them, What counsel give ye that we may answer this people, who have spoken to me, saying, Make the yoke which thy father did put upon us lighter?

And the young men that were grown up with him spake unto him, saying, Thus shalt thou speak unto this people that spake unto thee, saying, Thy father made our yoke heavy, but make thou it lighter unto us; thus shalt thou say unto them, My little finger shall be thicker than my father's loins.

And now whereas my father did lade you with a heavy yoke, I will add to your yoke: my father hath chastised you with whips, but I will chastise you with scorpions.

So Jeroboam and all the people came to Rehoboam the third day, as the king had appointed, saying, Come to me again the third day.

And the king answered the people roughly, and forsook the old men's counsel that they gave him;

And spake to them after the counsel of the young men, saying, My father made your yoke heavy, and I will add to your yoke: my father also chastised you with whips, but I will chastise you with scorpions.

Wherefore the king hearkened not unto the people; for the cause was from the LORD, that he might perform his saying, which the LORD spake by Ahijah the Shilonite unto Jeroboam the son of Nebat.

So when all Israel saw that the king hearkened not unto them, the people answered the king, saying, What portion have we in David? neither have we inheritance in the son of Jesse: to your tents, O Israel: now see to thine own house, David. So Israel departed unto their tents.

But as for the children of Israel which dwelt in the cities of Judah, Rehoboam reigned over them.

The Bible tells us of three and only three institutions that were created by God:

- **Family**
- **Government**
- **Church**

I would submit to you that there is a kind of liberty that we can possess only within the boundaries of one of those three institutions:

- **It is within my family I am free to reproduce faith**
- **It is within my government I am free to produce a livelihood**
- **It is within my church I am free to produce true worship of my Saviour**

Given that liberty is essentially tied up within these three institutions, it makes perfect sense that the enemy of liberty – the one who wants more than any other thing to enslave you to himself - would attack these institutions ferociously.

- **It happened in the days of Abraham when Sarah's proposal that Abraham have a child by Hagar nearly tore their family apart**
- **It happened in Isaac's family when Jacob and Esau grew (for a time) to hate each other so badly they had no communication for twenty years**
- **It happened in Jacob's family**
- **It happened in Moses' family**

- **It happened in Israel under Moses when, because of unbelief an, entire generation of Jews died before God gave them the Promised Land**
- **It happened under Joshua's leadership when, because of a misunderstanding with the two tribes who stayed on the other side of the Jordan, a civil war nearly broke out**
- **It happened in the rift between David and Saul – a seed of division was sown in Israel that bore its fruit when Solomon's son, Rehoboam became king**

It happened in the earliest days of our country's fight for independence when, even as the Declaration of Independence was receiving its finishing touches, the seed of disagreement concerning the issue of slavery threatened to rip apart our country before it was a country.

Most of us are familiar with the preamble of the Declaration, which says in part:

> "We hold these truths to be self-evident, that all men are created equal, that they are endowed by their Creator with certain unalienable rights, that among these are Life, Liberty, and the pursuit of Happiness."

The Declaration of Independence is meant to argue why the American's felt duty bound and morally justified to revolt against the British government. In that vein, the lion's share of the Declaration of Independence is a list of grievances they held against the King of England. Jefferson's original draft included an accusation against the king of creating an unjust situation in America by approving of slavery. Jefferson wrote against the king,

"He has waged cruel war against human nature itself, violating it's most sacred rights of life & liberty in the persons of a distant people who never offended him, captivating & carrying them into slavery in another hemisphere, or to incur miserable death in their transportation thither. This piratical warfare, the opprobrium of infidel powers, is the warfare of the CHRISTIAN king of Great Britain, determined to keep open a market where MEN should be bought & sold. He has prostituted his negative for suppressing every legislative attempt to prohibit or to restrain this execrable commerce: and that this assemblage of horrors might want no fact of distinguished die, he is now exciting those very people to rise in arms among us, and to purchase that liberty of which he has deprived them, & murdering the people upon whom he also obtruded them; thus paying off former crimes committed against the liberties of one people, with crimes which he urges them to commit against the lives of another."

The problem was that every one of the southern members of that congress, including Jefferson, was a slave owner. Congress tabled the debate over slavery until the "bigger" issue of Independence and the Revolutionary War was over. The debate was revived during the Constitutional Convention and was tabled until a Constitution of the United States could be ratified. The debate simmered through the first 75 years of our national history until, in the 1860's, it erupted into Civil War.

God has given us three and only three institutions for the advancement of liberty:

- **The family**
- **The government**
- **The church**

The enemy of liberty is mounting an all out attack on all three today.

ON THE FAMILY FRONT

I do not want to focus on the negatives this morning, but we do need to confront them. The Biblical family unit is threatened today by:

A. Slippery Ceremonies

Divorces are easy to get and people are getting them.

B. Premarital Promiscuity

Sexual relationships before and outside of marriage are so much the norm right now that the average person does not believe there is such a thing as sexual purity before marriage. And that is as true of the professing Christians as those who profess no faith at all.

C. LGBT Lies

Between the legalization homosexual marriage and the current Bruce Jenner popularity, Christians ought to be on their knees weeping in contrition before God.

The enemy's next assault is

ON THE NATIONAL FRONT

The United States has always been a land of great diversity
- **Diversity of faith**
- **Diversity of nationality**
- **Diversity of income**

The founding fathers didn't even really agree on politics. Some of them wanted George Washington to become a king. Some of them didn't want any central government at all.

Previous to the writing of the Constitution, some of the founding fathers wrote a series of articles called the Federalist Papers and an opposing group wrote a series of responses called the Anti-Federalist Papers. The controversy was so sharp that, in neither case, did the authors use their real names. It was common in those days for men who were political antagonists to take their gripes out on each other in a duel. Aaron Burr who was no less than the third Vice President of the United States shot and killed Alexander Hamilton, the first Secretary of the Treasury and one of the leading Generals in the Revolutionary War.

We have always had our differences. But those early fathers of our country agreed on this – they were Americans right or wrong.

What is going on in America today is not the same. We are disintegrating from the inside out.

A. We are allowing people to enter into our boarders who never intend to become citizens, who never plan to pay taxes, but who insist on ravaging our nation of its benefits.

B. Men and women elected to public offices not only disagree with long held policies of our country but express a hatred for the America way of life.

C. The founding fathers once printed money without possessing the capitol to back it.

The resulting inflation was so crippling that they sacrificed to pay their debt and passed a law making it illegal to ever make that mistake again. More modern leaders chose to reverse that law in the 1960's. America has been printing money not worth the paper it's on ever since. It will be our children and grandchildren who suffer the consequences[1] because no one is planning to sacrifice to pay any debt today.

Satan's third assault, of course is,

ON THE CHURCH FRONT

I do not mean to imply that it is only recently that Satan has begun to attack the local church.
- **Christ loved the church and gave Himself for it, therefore**
- **Satan hates the church and devoted himself against it**

Before the apostles had even passed away, certain men had "crept in unawares"[2] working havoc in the churches. By the third century the church had become married to the state and people were forced to worship God the way the government decreed. The monster created by the marriage of church and state became so corrupted that, by the 15th century even the loyal members of the church realized a protest was necessary. But the churches they created were none the better, still brutally persecuting those who would not worship:
- **Where**
- **When**
- **How**

they ordered.

As bad as things were when, in England, the country was tossed back and forth between the Catholics and the Protestants, each one killing off the other whenever they had the power to do so and both of them killing the Baptists and Dissenters, I believe things are much worse in America right now.

Our founding fathers, influenced by Baptist preachers of their day, envisioned a place where two preciously Baptist doctrines reigned preeminent:
- **Separation of church and state**
- **Individual soul liberty**

But while they hoped that every man would worship God according to the dictates of his or her own conscience, they could never have dreamed of a time when people would abandon the worship of God at all.

Thomas Paine was arguably one of the most influential men in our country's early history his writing of Common Sense and later The American Crisis served to catapult American sentiment in favor of Independence. But did you know that Paine died penniless and disreputably? Between 1794-1796, while in a French prison, Paine wrote what became his most famous [3] work at the time; the anti-Christian, anti-church, *The Age of Reason*. Paine "…returned to America [in 1802] on an invitation from Thomas Jefferson. Paine discovered that his contributions to the American Revolution had been all but eradicated due to his religious views…[4]" Only six people attended his funeral and everyone refused to bury him on American soil. No one knows whatever happened to his body. It was hauled to England at some point and, once claimed to have been seen in a farmer's barn.

Nobody then would have dreamed of the:
- **Disaffection**

- **Disrespect**
- **Disregard**

Concerning worship that is demonstrated in America today.

Conclusion:

I have to tell you, after spending all of this time complaining, I sure don't want to end my message there.

If we are going to identify problems, we ought to at least propose some solutions.

A. Pray for the healing of our land

2 Chronicles 7:14 KJV

If my people, which are called by my name, shall humble themselves, and pray, and seek my face, and turn from their wicked ways; then will I hear from heaven, and will forgive their sin, and will heal their land.

B. Study to show ourselves approved

2 Timothy 2:15 KJV

Study to shew thyself approved unto God, a workman that needeth not to be ashamed, rightly dividing the word of truth.

We can never say that we are free unless we are aware and educated. A person who is not a student of the Bible is a slave to whatever persuasion he holds, even if he believes it is no persuasion at all.

C. Practice Soul Liberty

John 4:24 KJV

God is a Spirit: and they that worship him must worship him in spirit and in truth.

That means worship. To claim you have the right to worship God according to the dictates of your own conscience, and then to skip out on worship altogether, is to abuse your right. No man ought to be forced to attend one church or the other.

But every man ought to find that place of worship he believes is most true to the Word of God and faithfully worship and serve God there.

D. Proclaim boldly the truths of this Word
1 Thessalonians 2:4 KJV
But as we were allowed of God to be put in trust with the gospel, even so we speak; not as pleasing men, but God, which trieth our hearts.

It has become apparent that, to even imply that Bruce Jenner is wrong for pretending to be a woman is considered "hate speech." I do not believe it will be long before it is illegal in America to say:
- **Homosexuality is sin**
- **Cross dressing is sin**
- **Abortion is sin**

I don't believe we have to say those things in a mean spirited way[5] but it does need to be said.

- **Persistently**
- **Persuasively**
- **Passionately**
- **Prayerfully**

At the same time we are preaching against sin, we must be promoting Jesus Christ:
- **Not religion**
- **Not rituals**

but a real and living relationship with Jesus Christ.

James 5:19-20 KJV
Brethren, if any of you do err from the truth, and one convert him;
Let him know, that he which converteth the sinner from the error of his way shall save a soul from death, and shall hide a multitude of sins.

[1] Assuming the country lasts until they are grown.
[2] Jude 1:4
[3] Infamous?
[4] http://www.ushistory.org/paine, accessed 6-6-15
[5] I will freely admit that it is often said in a mean spirited way.

Chapter Fifteen

JOIN OR DIE

1 Kings 12:1-17 KJV

And Rehoboam went to Shechem: for all Israel were come to Shechem to make him king.

And it came to pass, when Jeroboam the son of Nebat, who was yet in Egypt, heard of it, (for he was fled from the presence of king Solomon, and Jeroboam dwelt in Egypt;)

That they sent and called him. And Jeroboam and all the congregation of Israel came, and spake unto Rehoboam, saying,

Thy father made our yoke grievous: now therefore make thou the grievous service of thy father, and his heavy yoke which he put upon us, lighter, and we will serve thee.

And he said unto them, Depart yet for three days, then come again to me. And the people departed.

And king Rehoboam consulted with the old men, that stood before Solomon his father while he yet lived, and said, How do ye advise that I may answer this people?

And they spake unto him, saying, If thou wilt be a servant unto this people this day, and wilt serve them, and answer them, and speak good words to them, then they will be thy servants for ever.

But he forsook the counsel of the old men, which they had given him, and consulted with the young men that were grown up with him, and which stood before him:

And he said unto them, What counsel give ye that we may answer this people, who have spoken to me, saying, Make the yoke which thy father did put upon us lighter?

And the young men that were grown up with him spake unto him, saying, Thus shalt thou speak unto this people that spake unto thee, saying, Thy father made our yoke heavy, but make thou it lighter unto us; thus shalt thou say unto them, My little finger shall be thicker than my father's loins.

And now whereas my father did lade you with a heavy yoke, I will add to your yoke: my father hath chastised you with whips, but I will chastise you with scorpions.

So Jeroboam and all the people came to Rehoboam the third day, as the king had appointed, saying, Come to me again the third day.

And the king answered the people roughly, and forsook the old men's counsel that they gave him;
And spake to them after the counsel of the young men, saying, My father made your yoke heavy, and I will add to your yoke: my father also chastised you with whips, but I will chastise you with scorpions.
Wherefore the king hearkened not unto the people; for the cause was from the LORD, that he might perform his saying, which the LORD spake by Ahijah the Shilonite unto Jeroboam the son of Nebat.
So when all Israel saw that the king hearkened not unto them, the people answered the king, saying, What portion have we in David? neither have we inheritance in the son of Jesse: to your tents, O Israel: now see to thine own house, David. So Israel departed unto their tents.
But as for the children of Israel which dwelt in the cities of Judah, Rehoboam reigned over them.

American history is fairly flush with flags having historic, patriotic and inspirational significance:

1. The "Grand Union Flag"[1] (also known as the "Continental Colours," the "Congress Flag," the "Cambridge Flag," and the "First Navy Ensign") is considered to be the first national flag of the United States of America. – until 1777. The inclusion of the Union Jack was intended to point out that the Colonists did not intend to separate from Britain

2. The Betsy Ross flag is an early design of the flag of the United States. The flag was designed during the American Revolution. The distinctive feature of the Betsy Ross flag is, of course, the arrangement of the stars in a circle.

3. The national flag of the United States of America, often referred to as the American flag, consists of thirteen equal horizontal stripes of red (top and bottom) alternating with white, with a blue rectangle in the union bearing fifty small white, five pointed stars representing each of the United States.

4. October of 1831 saw the battle of Gonzales when Mexican forces came to the town of Gonzales to confiscate their small swivel canon used for the defense of the town. As a symbol of

defiance, before the battle, the people of Gonzales had fashioned this flag, "Come and Take It".

5. Though not originally a flag[2], one of the most famous symbols in American history is this political cartoon, "Join or Die", published in 1754. The cartoon appeared along with Franklin's editorial about the "disunited state" of the colonies and helped make his point about the importance of colonial unity. It was first used to symbolize the colonies' need to join with Britain in the French and Indian war. It later became a symbol of colonial freedom during the Revolutionary War.

The American colonies were, by their very construction, very individualistic states of government.

- **Each colony had been established at a different period in history**
- **Each colony had been granted its own charter by the king of England and with its own stated purpose**
- **Each colony had created its own government (constitution)**
- **Each colony had its own church tradition (its established state church)**

They were all British subjects but each one had had its own disputes with their mother country that had initially led them to move here. And, had they stayed in England these one hundred forty or so years, they would have been ardent opponents of one another's politics and religion. That they were on this continent hardly changed that. With his cartoon, Franklin was asserting that the liberty their forefathers had risked everything to find in America was threatened unless they could find a way to work in harmony together.

Liberty is always threatened through division.

That's why the New Testament is filled with verses urging us to Ephesians 4:3 KJV

Endeavouring to keep the unity of the Spirit in the bond of peace.

A significant portion of the Old Testament is a description of Israel in a divided state.

Division was the fault of:

DOING WHAT WAS RIGHT IN THEIR OWN EYES

Judges 21:25 KJV

In those days there was no king in Israel: every man did that which was right in his own eyes.

A phrase similar to this is found in three other places in the book of Judges.

- **Moses was dead**
- **Joshua was dead**
- **The judges were, for the most part, temporary and regional leaders**

There was, of course, the Tabernacle and the High Priest, representing God's leadership in their lives, but he was ineffective to say the least. Disunity had overtaken Israel.

- **No one was listening to God (and least not very many of them)**
- **No one was obeying the Word of God (the best unifier that has ever existed)**

Everyone was just doing what they wanted to do and what they thought was right. And because they were not unified, they kept getting attacked. Many times, these attacks might have been avoided if only they would have presented a unified front from the beginning.

The devil has done a great job of creating a world of disunity within Christianity.

- **We have varying denominations**
- **We have differing doctrines**
- **We have divisive para-church groups**
- **We have Christians who are not united with a local church**

It has created an environment where the world, the flesh and the devil feel perfectly free to attack our faith at their will. I do not believe we ought to all just join hands and love one another; thereby creating unity. A solid union that can stand against Satan is one that is built around the truths of the Bible.

- **Germany had unity around Hitler**
- **Russia had unity around Stalin**

Unity is important, but most important is that the unity be built around what is right, what is just, what is true.

Because they did what was right in their own eyes, they made the mistake of:

DEMANDING A KING THROUGH POPULARITY RATHER THAN SPIRITUAL MEANS

1 Samuel 8:5-9 KJV

And said unto him, Behold, thou art old, and thy sons walk not in thy ways: now make us a king to judge us like all the nations.

But the thing displeased Samuel, when they said, Give us a king to judge us. And Samuel prayed unto the LORD.

And the LORD said unto Samuel, Hearken unto the voice of the people in all that they say unto thee: for they have not rejected thee, but they have rejected me, that I should not reign over them.

According to all the works which they have done since the day that I brought them up out of Egypt even unto this day, wherewith they have forsaken me, and served other gods, so do they also unto thee.

Now therefore hearken unto their voice: howbeit yet protest solemnly unto them, and shew them the manner of the king that shall reign over them.

With Samuel came a new sort of leadership in Israel; the prophet. Samuel served as a judge, but he was more than that – he was a man of God and a man of God's Word. But the people were not satisfied with having a man of God leading them. They wanted something else; they wanted what everyone else had. The resulting king – one that they forced upon themselves – was:

- **Tall**
- **Impressive looking**
- **Even seemed to be a believer**

He was very popular. The only problem was, he wasn't the will of God.

Choosing a king at this stage in their nation and without the express consent of the Lord set Israel up for the division that eventually caused their nation to disintegrate. Now isn't that interesting? Doing what everyone else was doing led to Israel's disunity rather than unity. The greatest unifier in the world is separation from the world around the person of Jesus Christ and the truths He gives us in the Word of God.

A local church is filled with people of all sorts of varying

- **Backgrounds**
- **Interests**
- **Educations**
- **Social positions**

Yet, when we all focus on our identification with Christ and not with the world – we are one body.

A third factor leading to Israel's division was,

JEALOUSY OVER THE ONE GOD HAD CHOSEN

1 Samuel 18:8-10 KJV

And Saul was very wroth, and the saying displeased him; and he said, They have ascribed unto David ten thousands, and to me they have ascribed but thousands: and what can he have more but the kingdom? And Saul eyed David from that day and forward.
And it came to pass on the morrow, that the evil spirit from God came upon Saul, and he prophesied in the midst of the house: and David played with his hand, as at other times: and there was a javelin in Saul's hand.

This spirit of jealousy existed not only in Saul but continued on in those who would later become the ten northern tribes. During the rebellion, of David's own son Absalom, the Bible says that,

2 Samuel 15:6 KJV

… Absalom stole the hearts of the men of Israel.

He didn't steal the hearts of the men of Judah. But the men of Israel, these were the ones who did not immediately follow King David after Saul died.

2 Samuel 2:4 KJV

And the men of Judah came, and there they anointed David king over the house of Judah. And they told David, saying, That the men of Jabesh-gilead were they that buried Saul.

2 Samuel 2:8-9 KJV

But Abner the son of Ner, captain of Saul's host, took Ish-bosheth the son of Saul, and brought him over to Mahanaim;
And made him king over Gilead, and over the Ashurites, and over Jezreel, and over Ephraim, and over Benjamin, and over all Israel.

When David first became King he only ruled over Judah while Saul's son, Ishbosheth ruled over Israel. This division of the kingdom lasted seven years so that, really, the two kingdoms that were established when Rehoboam followed the counsel of his friends really already existed in the jealous hearts of Israel the whole time King David was on the throne.

The Israelites were jealous over the one God had chosen. They liked their guy.

And because of it they had,

Good men chose the wrong side because they were loyal.

2 Samuel 2:8-9 KJV
But Abner the son of Ner, captain of Saul's host, took Ish-bosheth the son of Saul, and brought him over to Mahanaim;
And made him king over Gilead, and over the Ashurites, and over Jezreel, and over Ephraim, and over Benjamin, and over all Israel.

King David agrees with me that Abner was a good man.
2 Samuel 3:38 KJV
And the king said unto his servants, Know ye not that there is a prince and a great man fallen this day in Israel?

Abner was a good man, but he was loyal to the wrong king.

I have met some very good people who are:
- **Loyal to the wrong church denomination**
- **Loyal to the wrong political agenda**
- **Loyal to the wrong cultural ideas**
- **Loyal to the wrong traditions of rearing children**
- **Loyal to the wrong friendships**

Those loyalties tend to create division
- **In their lives**
- **In their family**
- **In their church**

and those same loyalties will eventually cause them personal devastation. Some of them might seem like good causes, but they create a conflict in the heart and home because they are not genuinely biblical loyalties.

Finally, division was created in Israel because of

Once in a while something would happen in David's reign, like the rebellion of Absalom that would cause that jealous spirit to rise up all over again:

2 Samuel 16:5-8 KJV

And when king David came to Bahurim, behold, thence came out a man of the family of the house of Saul, whose name was Shimei, the son of Gera: he came forth, and cursed still as he came.

And he cast stones at David, and at all the servants of king David: and all the people and all the mighty men were on his right hand and on his left.

And thus said Shimei when he cursed, Come out, come out, thou bloody man, and thou man of Belial:

The LORD hath returned upon thee all the blood of the house of Saul, in whose stead thou hast reigned; and the LORD hath delivered the kingdom into the hand of Absalom thy son: and, behold, thou art taken in thy mischief, because thou art a bloody man.

The case of Shimei is a truly sad one. It is sad first of all because:

A. He had held on to this obvious bitterness all through the years of David's reign

Hebrews 12:15 KJV says

Looking diligently lest any man fail of the grace of God; lest any root of bitterness springing up trouble you, and thereby many be defiled;

Shimei had held on to this "root of bitterness" for years and years.

Who knows?

- **Maybe he had shouted "God save the king" and David's coronation**
- **Maybe he had served in David's army at some point in his life**
- **Maybe he had gone on quietly doing his work, hoping no one could sense the corruption in his own heart**

- **Maybe it was only in the privacy of his own home and among the members of his own family that he expressed his hatred for King David**

But then came that day when David's own son turned against him.

- **Shimei thought he saw his opportunity**
- **He could hold his bitterness in no longer**

He spilled out what really was always there.

Sometimes a person will go years smiling at people, pretending to care and be a part of what God is doing in a church, burying deeply inside them what they really believe. But one day the pressure gets too great and all of that garbage boils out –

- **They are mad at everybody**
- **They pour it out without restraint**

What comes out is not something new. It is what has always been in their heart. It has been slowly poisoning them and probably those who are the closest to them.

The story of Shimei is sad secondly,

B. Because David forgave him but he still held on to the bitterness

2 Samuel 19:16-23 KJV

And Shimei the son of Gera, a Benjamite, which was of Bahurim, hasted and came down with the men of Judah to meet king David.

And there were a thousand men of Benjamin with him, and Ziba the servant of the house of Saul, and his fifteen sons and his twenty servants with him; and they went over Jordan before the king.

And there went over a ferry boat to carry over the king's household, and to do what he thought good. And Shimei the son of Gera fell down before the king, as he was come over Jordan;

And said unto the king, Let not my lord impute iniquity unto me, neither do thou remember that which thy servant did perversely the day that my lord the king went out of Jerusalem, that the king should take it to his heart.

For thy servant doth know that I have sinned: therefore, behold, I am come the first this day of all the house of Joseph to go down to meet my lord the king.
But Abishai the son of Zeruiah answered and said, Shall not Shimei be put to death for this, because he cursed the LORD'S anointed?
And David said, What have I to do with you, ye sons of Zeruiah, that ye should this day be adversaries unto me? shall there any man be put to death this day in Israel? for do not I know that I am this day king over Israel?
Therefore the king said unto Shimei, Thou shalt not die. And the king sware unto him.

The conflict between Absalom and King David did not end the way Shimei thought it would. David won. Here comes Shimei groveling before David, hoping to save his own life. And it worked. Against the advice of Abishai, David spared Shimei's life. He had a new lease on life; a fresh opportunity. But his heart had not changed and I suspect that David knew it. When he turned the kingdom over to Solomon David confided,
1 Kings 2:8-9 KJV
And, behold, thou hast with thee Shimei the son of Gera, a Benjamite of Bahurim, which cursed me with a grievous curse in the day when I went to Mahanaim: but he came down to meet me at Jordan, and I sware to him by the LORD, saying, I will not put thee to death with the sword.
Now therefore hold him not guiltless: for thou art a wise man, and knowest what thou oughtest to do unto him; but his hoar head bring thou down to the grave with blood.

Solomon agreed to allow Shimei to live so long as he never left the city of Jerusalem again. Shimei agreed but three years later he had a couple of slaves who ran away and he chased after them. When he got back to Jerusalem, Solomon had him slain. He never learned to be loyal to the king God set over Israel. It cost him his life.

Over the years I have known a number of people who have that bitter heart who will, once in a while subdue it, maybe even confess it to God, but never dig out that root and let God have full control of them. Let me tell you, we can play the part of a Christian as long as we want, but as long as there is something in our heart we will not give over to God;

- **Something we thing we deserve**
- **Something we think we can hold without hindering our Christianity**

Then we are deceiving ourselves.

"No man can serve two masters" the division that attempting to do so will create in your heart

- **Will divide your family**
- **Will divide you from your church**
- **Will divide you from peace and liberty before God**

[1] The descriptions of each of these flags have been drawn from Wikipedia pages and edited for this message.
[2] This is considered the first political cartoon in American history.

Chapter Sixteen

KEYS TO LIBERTY

Leviticus 25:8-12 KJV

And thou shalt number seven sabbaths of years unto thee, seven times seven years; and the space of the seven sabbaths of years shall be unto thee forty and nine years.

Then shalt thou cause the trumpet of the jubile to sound on the tenth day of the seventh month, in the day of atonement shall ye make the trumpet sound throughout all your land.

And ye shall hallow the fiftieth year, and proclaim liberty throughout all the land unto all the inhabitants thereof: it shall be a jubile unto you; and ye shall return every man unto his possession, and ye shall return every man unto his family.

A jubile shall that fiftieth year be unto you: ye shall not sow, neither reap that which groweth of itself in it, nor gather the grapes in it of thy vine undressed.

For it is the jubile; it shall be holy unto you: ye shall eat the increase thereof out of the field.

We, as people, are easily fooled about what things are important and what things are not. Oftentimes we place great emphasis on things that we believe have HUGE eternal consequence and neglect, or nearly so, things that GOD places the most emphasis upon. Jesus put it like this:

Matthew 23:23 KJV

Woe unto you, scribes and Pharisees, hypocrites! for ye pay tithe of mint and anise and cummin, and have omitted the weightier matters of the law, judgment, mercy, and faith: these ought ye to have done, and not to leave the other undone.

I suspect that when we get to heaven we are going to find out that a lot of things that we thought really mattered – really didn't matter as much as we thought. Unfortunately I believe we are also going to find out that we didn't put much attention to things that God holds priceless.

Israel offers us an illustration of that principle. One of the commandments God placed upon them prior to entering the Promised Land is that, every seventh year they were to give their land a rest from farming. Then, every fiftieth year they were to "go big" and make it a jubilee.

- **Forgive all their debtors**
- **Release all their servants**
- **Restore to everyone their original possessions**

It was a big deal.

So that, when they were finally taken captives by Babylon, God said that they would be judged specifically seventy years, giving the Promised Land, it's rightful Sabbath rests that Israel had just ignored for 490 years.

Our text is God's original command concerning those Sabbath rests for the land, and the practice of the fiftieth year of jubilee. Notice that God says on the year of jubilee, they were to "proclaim liberty throughout all the land".

I find in verse 10, four keys to true liberty.

IT IS A HALLOWED THING

And ye shall hallow the fiftieth year and proclaim liberty.

To hallow something is:
- **To make it holy**
- **To make it sacred**
- **To dedicate it to God**
- **To revere it**

God was talking about an event in the life of Israel, the fiftieth year. But the reason the Jubilee year matters is because it focused the attention of the people on their liberty.

- **Liberty**
- **Freedom**

is a SACRED thing.

That's what the founders of our country pledged their lives, their fortunes and their sacred honor toward. That's why innumerable multitudes of Baptist and Anabaptist forefathers endured brutal:

- **Capture**
- **Torture**
- **Execution**

Liberty as a citizen, but more so, liberty of conscience to seek God in spirit and in truth and to worship Him as He reveals Himself to you .

That is a hallowed, sacred thing.

IT IS A UNIVERSAL THING

...proclaim liberty throughout all the land unto all the inhabitants thereof...

I draw your attention to the two times you see the word, "all".

Thomas Jefferson wrote, and the world has endorsed it as true; "We hold these truths self evident, that all men are created equal..." Jefferson personally struggled with this truth, knowing that in his own world, in his own life, not all men were treated equally. Jefferson's Declaration of Independence was published and read all over the world – especially all over the continent, and as it was read both the women and the blacks in America took note of that three letter word; all.

Four score and seven years after America won her liberty, she found herself fighting once again for liberty. In many respects we have never stopped fighting because we have never perfectly embraced the "all men" clause of the Declaration.

Much more important than physical, national or ethnical liberty, is the liberty of the soul. That all men and women, no matter where they are and no matter what their backgrounds might experience:
- **Freedom from the judgment of sin**
- **Freedom from the snare of Satan**
- **Freedom from an eternity is hell**

That is a fight we must never surrender!

IT IS A PERSONAL THING

...and ye shall return every man unto his possession...

I want to key off the two words "his possession" for a moment and remind this congregation that individual soul liberty is a personal thing.

- **It's not a national thing**
- **It's not even a congregational thing**

- **Nobody is going to go to heaven because they are citizens of America**
- **Nobody is going to go to heaven because they attend this Baptist church**

- **Nobody goes to heaven because their parents are Christians**
- **Nobody goes to heaven because they were drug to church services all of their life**

This is what all of those Baptists and Anabaptists meant to teach when they suffered and died for their faith – a saving relationship with God,
- **Cannot be forced upon you by your country**
- **Cannot be bequeathed to you by your church**

It must be your own personal possession or it is no good to you at all.

IT IS A FAMILIAL THING

...and ye shall return every man unto his family.

Our relationship with the Lord is always a personal possession. No one walks with the Lord for us. On the other hand, it is unreasonable to believe that we walk with the Lord alone.

A. I want to reach my family

John 1:40-41 KJV

One of the two which heard John speak, and followed him, was Andrew, Simon Peter's brother.
He first findeth his own brother Simon, and saith unto him, We have found the Messias, which is, being interpreted, the Christ.

It's the most normal thing in the world, when you have found something amazing to tell those you care the most about it first.

B. Becoming a believer restores us to the family of God

So that there is a relationship that happens to those of us who are Christians that sometimes becomes even closer than blood family.

Conclusion

Israel missed the importance of the Sabbath rest for the land, probably viewing it as an insignificant part of their faith. We want to make sure that we do not miss just how important liberty to worship Christ is to us.

- **That you can open a Bible and search it for yourself**
- **That you can pray and hear from God yourself**

- **That you can come to a church where souls of like mind worship together**

These are not trivial things we ought to take or leave as we please.

Chapter Seventeen

TARLETON'S QUARTER

Ephesians 4:20-27 KJV

But ye have not so learned Christ;

If so be that ye have heard him, and have been taught by him, as the truth is in Jesus:

That ye put off concerning the former conversation the old man, which is corrupt according to the deceitful lusts;

And be renewed in the spirit of your mind;

And that ye put on the new man, which after God is created in righteousness and true holiness.

Wherefore putting away lying, speak every man truth with his neighbour: for we are members one of another.

Be ye angry, and sin not: let not the sun go down upon your wrath:

Neither give place to the devil.

The Revolution that won our country's independence began in the New England Colonies:

- **Massachusetts**
- **Connecticut**
- **New York**
- **New Jersey**
- **Pennsylvania**

Very important battles were waged in those northern areas. But some of the most bloody, brutal and influential battles were fought in the southern colonies; Virginia and South Carolina especially.

In the days of the American Revolution armies liked to think they fought under "civilized rules".

- **Officers on either side respected each other**
- **You weren't supposed to really shoot at the officers**
- **When a white flag was raised, you stopped shooting**
- **Etc.**

War in those southern colonies was not so civil. One of the most brutal and infamous officers in the Revolution was a British Lieutenant Colonel named Banastre Tarleton, nicknamed "Bloody Ban" and "The Butcher." His most notorious act took place in what became known as the Battle of Waxhaws; Americans called it "Tarleton's Quarter".

Tartleton, with 149 mounted soldiers, overtook a detachment of 350 Virginian Continental soldiers led by a man named Abraham Buford. A battle ensued and at some point, Buford raised a white flag of surrender. The story gets muddled from here – depending on whose side you listen to. At about the same time as the white flag was raised, Tarleton's horse was shot out from under him. This sent him and his men into a rage. They attacked the Continentals, who believed they were under a flag of truce, and began murdering them, stabbing the wounded where they lay.

When word got out about what happened, the phrase "Tarleton's Quarter" became a sort of rallying cry for the Americans like "Remember the Alamo" so that, in a battle that followed, when the Americans had the upper hand and the British asked for "quarters" or conditions for surrender, the American's response was, "Tarleton's Quarter"
- **No conditions**
- **No mercy**
- **No surrender**

fight to the death.

It is considered a war crime to refuse to quarter, or house, prisoners of war. But I want to use the phrase to point out three enemies the Bible says we must give no quarter to.
- **We cannot give them mercy**
- **We cannot let them have any place in our life**

We must fight them to the death lest they be the death of us.

IDLE WORDS

Matthew 12:36-37 KJV
But I say unto you, That every idle word that men shall speak, they shall give account thereof in the day of judgment.
For by thy words thou shalt be justified, and by thy words thou shalt be condemned.

I doubt that we put as much stock in the importance of our words as we should. The Lord said that we are both justified and condemned by our words.

It is with the mouth that we are saved:
Romans 10:9-10 KJV
That if thou shalt confess with thy mouth the Lord Jesus, and shalt believe in thine heart that God hath raised him from the dead, thou shalt be saved.
For with the heart man believeth unto righteousness; and with the mouth confession is made unto salvation.

Who could ever overestimate the value of the well-spoken word to the spiritual well being of others?

The Bible says of the Apostle Paul,
 Acts 14:1 KJV
And it came to pass in Iconium, that they went both together into the synagogue of the Jews, and so spake, that a great multitude both of the Jews and also of the Greeks believed.

Romans 10:14-15 KJV says
How then shall they call on him in whom they have not believed? and how shall they believe in him of whom they have not heard? and how shall they hear without a preacher?
And how shall they preach, except they be sent? as it is written, How beautiful are the feet of them that preach the gospel of peace, and bring glad tidings of good things!

So valuable is the word to the eternal souls of men that Jesus Christ is called The Word

John 1:14 KJV

And the Word was made flesh, and dwelt among us, (and we beheld his glory, the glory as of the only begotten of the Father,) full of grace and truth.

1 John 5:7 KJV

For there are three that bear record in heaven, the Father, the Word, and the Holy Ghost: and these three are one.

On the other hand, words can

- **Damage friendships**
- **Destroy relationships**
- **Decimate churches**
- **Damn souls to hell**

James 3:3-12 KJV

Behold, we put bits in the horses' mouths, that they may obey us; and we turn about their whole body.

Behold also the ships, which though they be so great, and are driven of fierce winds, yet are they turned about with a very small helm, whithersoever the governor listeth.

Even so the tongue is a little member, and boasteth great things. Behold, how great a matter a little fire kindleth!

And the tongue is a fire, a world of iniquity: so is the tongue among our members, that it defileth the whole body, and setteth on fire the course of nature; and it is set on fire of hell.

For every kind of beasts, and of birds, and of serpents, and of things in the sea, is tamed, and hath been tamed of mankind:

But the tongue can no man tame; it is an unruly evil, full of deadly poison.

Therewith bless we God, even the Father; and therewith curse we men, which are made after the similitude of God.

Out of the same mouth proceedeth blessing and cursing. My brethren, these things ought not so to be.

Doth a fountain send forth at the same place sweet water and bitter?

Can the fig tree, my brethren, bear olive berries? either a vine, figs? so can no fountain both yield salt water and fresh.

We can use our words to bring others to a saving knowledge of Jesus Christ or to drive them forever away from Jesus Christ. Therefore we must give idle words no quarter. We cannot afford to let words slip out of our mouth without having thought them through and weighed their impact upon others.

Give your idle words "Tarleton's Quarter."

THE DEEDS OF THE FLESH

Ephesians 4:20-27 KJV
But ye have not so learned Christ;
If so be that ye have heard him, and have been taught by him, as the truth is in Jesus:
That ye put off concerning the former conversation the old man, which is corrupt according to the deceitful lusts;
And be renewed in the spirit of your mind;
And that ye put on the new man, which after God is created in righteousness and true holiness.
Wherefore putting away lying, speak every man truth with his neighbour: for we are members one of another.
Be ye angry, and sin not: let not the sun go down upon your wrath:
Neither give place to the devil.

The passage I have selected here begins with the name of Christ and ends with the devil. Those of us who know Jesus Christ need to "put off the old man" and "put on the new man".

The new man is characterized by:
- **Truth**
- **Righteousness**
- **Holiness**

The old man is characterized by:
- **Corruption**
- **Lust**
- **Deceit**
- **Anger**

The final phrase says – give no "place to the devil". It literally means, "no quarter".
- **No mercy**
- **No concession**
- **No clemency**

For us, concerning the working of the flesh and the old man, the sins that were so much a part of our life before we got saved, we have to completely kill it off. We are to mortify the deeds of the flesh. We can't make excuses for our sin and old life. We need to turn from it completely, not for salvation – that is all won through Jesus Christ, but for victory in our personal growth.

A FALSE GOSPEL

Galatians 1:6-9 KJV

I marvel that ye are so soon removed from him that called you into the grace of Christ unto another gospel:
Which is not another; but there be some that trouble you, and would pervert the gospel of Christ.
But though we, or an angel from heaven, preach any other gospel unto you than that which we have preached unto you, let him be accursed.
As we said before, so say I now again, If any man preach any other gospel unto you than that ye have received, let him be accursed.

Probably the most challenging place any Christian can come to in his life is:
- **When they KNOW the true Gospel and then**
- **To deny that any other gospel is valid**

Some of the nicest people I have ever met:

- **Believe in a different god than the one avowed to us in the Bible and have**
- **Trusted a different Christ than the one affirmed to us in the Bible**

They are nice people and I like them very much. In many cases I agree with them about several important issues. But the Gospel they preach is not only different than ours, it is an accursed gospel.

- **It is a lie**
- **It is from hell**
- **It will send souls to eternal torment in hell**

It cannot be countenanced. We must give it no quarter.
2 John 1:7-11 KJV
For many deceivers are entered into the world, who confess not that Jesus Christ is come in the flesh. This is a deceiver and an antichrist.
Look to yourselves, that we lose not those things which we have wrought, but that we receive a full reward.
Whosoever transgresseth, and abideth not in the doctrine of Christ, hath not God. He that abideth in the doctrine of Christ, he hath both the Father and the Son.
If there come any unto you, and bring not this doctrine, receive him not into your house, neither bid him God speed:
For he that biddeth him God speed is partaker of his evil deeds.

See in this verse the two parts: First is the situation of the person who brings this false gospel. They are lost and bound for hell. Our concern for them must be their soul. To give a place for their message is to give it legitimacy in their minds – something we must never do, for their sake.

But then see the situation of the person who gives the false doctrine quarter.
The Bible says that he has become a partaker in his evil deeds.

- If you let them in your house
- If you let them tell you what they believe
- If you let them teach you their false doctrines
- If you send them on their way believing they do God's work

In other words,

- If you give them quarter

You have become a part of the evil of their false doctrine.

It is the opposite of what Paul told the Philippians; because they had given to help him, they had received fruit to their account in heaven. If we give any place for those who preach a different gospel, a different Christ and a different salvation than our own; we then become accountable for the heresy they preach and the souls they send to hell. Blood is on our hands.

Conclusion:

There are some things we just cannot allow to survive

- The idle word
- The fleshly deed
- The false gospel

- I slay the idle word by speaking only those things that are "seasoned with grace"
- I slay the fleshly deed by renewing my spirit in the Word of God and by putting on the New Man which is obedient to Christ
- I slay the false gospel by knowing and earnestly preaching the true Gospel

Chapter Eighteen

FREEDOM IN SURRENDER

Jeremiah 38:17 KJV

Then said Jeremiah unto Zedekiah, Thus saith the LORD, the God of hosts, the God of Israel; If thou wilt assuredly go forth unto the king of Babylon's princes, then thy soul shall live, and this city shall not be burned with fire; and thou shalt live, and thine house:

America's victory overcame as an absolute shock to the English soldier. In the eyes of the British the Americans were:

- **So backwards**
- **So uncivilized**
- **So without refinement class and polish**

that even when they surrendered, they could not accept that they had been bettered by their betters.

As their soldiers marched out to surrender their weapons the English band played a tuned called "The World Turned Upside Down". The official surrender ceremony in those days involved the commanding officer of the surrendering force to surrender his sword to the commanding officer of the Victor. In this case, Lord Cornwallis was so embarrassed at losing to the Americans that he did the unthinkable (he would never have considered do this had he respected the Americans) and refused to participate, sending a subordinate officer, General Charles O'Hara in his place. That officer attempted to surrender his sword, not to General Washington but to the French General Rochambeau. Rochambeau refused, insisting the sword go to the American General. Washington refused it as well, having a General Benjamin Lincoln accept the sword since it was a subordinate officer surrendering it.

As much as they may have hated losing to America – it was, in many ways, a liberating thing:

- **For England as they could stop spending massive amounts of money financing their war against America**
- **For the British soldier as his combat days were, at least for this war, over**
- **Banastre Tarleton, Americans called him "Bloody Ban"**

This monster on the battlefield returned to England, was promoted to general and began a successful career in politics.

- **Lord Cornwallis was criticized for his role in the southern campaign of the American Revolution but still went on in a successful military career in India, France, Russia and Ireland**
- **Every one of the major British officers returned home to more or less successful careers**

The subject of liberty is a principle doctrine from cover to cover of the Bible.

- **Historic Israel fought for it**
- **The Apostles taught about it**
- **Jesus set soul at liberty**
- **Where the Holy Spirit is, there is liberty**

So it should strike us strange that two of the most important moments in the life of Israel both had to do with their enslavement.

- **First, in Egypt**
- **Next, in Babylon**

Notice a few contrasts between these two periods of captivity:

Egypt	**Babylon**
-Entered in peacefully, left violently	-Entered in violently, left peacefully
-Entered because the land had quit producing	-Entered because they had not given the land rest from producing
-Lasted over 400 years	-Began after over 400 years in their kingdom

Jeremiah's job was to preach a message that seemed almost opposite of what Israel automatically thought was God's will for them. Jeremiah's message was that, at this point in Israel's history, their freedom would come, not in standing up to fight, but in giving in – in surrender.

Sometimes, the very greatest freedom comes, not from fighting – but from surrender.

SURRENDER YOUR WILL TO GOD'S

Matthew 26:36-39 KJV
Then cometh Jesus with them unto a place called Gethsemane, and saith unto the disciples, Sit ye here, while I go and pray yonder.
And he took with him Peter and the two sons of Zebedee, and began to be sorrowful and very heavy.
Then saith he unto them, My soul is exceeding sorrowful, even unto death: tarry ye here, and watch with me.
And he went a little further, and fell on his face, and prayed, saying, O my Father, if it be possible, let this cup pass from me: nevertheless not as I will, but as thou wilt.

It is without question that the greatest example of surrendering one's will to God the Father, is Jesus Christ in the Garden of Gethsemene. Can you imagine that Jesus would have needed to do that? His will is the Father's as He and the Father are one.

- **There is nothing that Jesus would have wanted that God the Father would not have wanted as well**
- **There is nothing that God the Father would have wanted that Jesus would not have wanted as well**

Jesus is the express image of the Father
- **In deed**
- **In word**
- **In power**
- **In sovereignty**
- **In infinity**

Jesus said that he that had seen Him had seen the Father. And yet Jesus prayed to His Heavenly Father, *"…nevertheless not my will, but thine, be done."*

I believe that prayer was offered and is here recorded for our benefit. If the Son of Man ever needed to surrender His will to the Father, how much more do we need to do that same.

The exact antithesis of this is Lucifer and his famous "I wills": Isaiah 14:12-14 KJV
How art thou fallen from heaven, O Lucifer, son of the morning! how art thou cut down to the ground, which didst weaken the nations!
For thou hast said in thine heart, I will ascend into heaven, I will exalt my throne above the stars of God: I will sit also upon the mount of the congregation, in the sides of the north:
I will ascend above the heights of the clouds; I will be like the most High.

The will of man, not surrendered to Christ, is always Satanic.

- **It might be your will to do a good thing**
- **It might be your will to live a valuable life**
- **It might be your will to serve good causes**

But if it is:

- **Your will and not**
- **God's will it is**
- **The devil's will**

- **Sometimes people choose to serve God one way or another as an excuse for not surrendering to God's precise will**
- **Someone will promise to give God lots of money instead of being a preacher**
- **Someone else will promise to teach a Sunday school class instead of being a missionary**

- **One person might promise to be a pastor instead of going to a foreign field**

- Another person will promise to be a missionary instead of pastoring a church in his own town

A. God's will is always holiest

Isaiah 6:1-3 KJV

In the year that king Uzziah died I saw also the Lord sitting upon a throne, high and lifted up, and his train filled the temple.

Above it stood the seraphims: each one had six wings; with twain he covered his face, and with twain he covered his feet, and with twain he did fly.

And one cried unto another, and said, Holy, holy, holy, is the LORD of hosts: the whole earth is full of his glory.

B. God's will is always highest

Isaiah 55:8-9 KJV

For my thoughts are not your thoughts, neither are your ways my ways, saith the LORD.

For as the heavens are higher than the earth, so are my ways higher than your ways, and my thoughts than your thoughts.

C. God's will is always happiest

John 15:11 KJV

These things have I spoken unto you, that my joy might remain in you, and that your joy might be full.

- You will never regret obeying the will of God for your life
- I guarantee you that you will one day regret NOT obeying the will of God for your life

Once people do surrender to God's will, one of the first things that they say is that they have been "fighting" it for a while. Note the word, "fight".

- Do you suppose anyone ever wins a fight with God?
- Do you suppose anyone really enjoys being in a fight?

- Ask Mohammed Ali
- Ask George Foreman

Ask them if, in the middle of their boxing match, "Are you having fun right now?" The answer is "No." There is nothing fun about a fight.

- **They get an income from fighting**
- **They get fame from fighting**
- **They get filled with adrenalin from fighting**

But they can never say that they get great joy from fighting. Joy comes when we surrender our will to God.

There is freedom when you,

SURRENDER YOUR MEMBERS TO RIGHTEOUSNESS

Romans 6:12-22 KJV

Let not sin therefore reign in your mortal body, that ye should obey it in the lusts thereof.

Neither yield ye your members as instruments of unrighteousness unto sin: but yield yourselves unto God, as those that are alive from the dead, and your members as instruments of righteousness unto God.

For sin shall not have dominion over you: for ye are not under the law, but under grace.

What then? shall we sin, because we are not under the law, but under grace? God forbid.

Know ye not, that to whom ye yield yourselves servants to obey, his servants ye are to whom ye obey; whether of sin unto death, or of obedience unto righteousness?

But God be thanked, that ye were the servants of sin, but ye have obeyed from the heart that form of doctrine which was delivered you.

Being then made free from sin, ye became the servants of righteousness.

I speak after the manner of men because of the infirmity of your flesh: for as ye have yielded your members servants to uncleanness and to iniquity unto iniquity; even so now yield your members servants to righteousness unto holiness.

For when ye were the servants of sin, ye were free from righteousness. What fruit had ye then in those things whereof ye are now ashamed? for the end of those things is death.

But now being made free from sin, and become servants to God, ye have your fruit unto holiness, and the end everlasting life.

You speak with anyone whose life is controlled by an addiction and they will tell you there is no freedom in it.
- **A young person might take up smoking because they think it makes them in charge of their life**
- **A person might start drinking because it makes them feel free from some problem in their life**
- **A person might start using drugs because it makes them fit in with the people around them**

But you ask them down the road if they are free….
- **They wake up every morning with their addiction on their mind**
- **They have to plan activities so there is a time and a place to give in to their addiction**
- **They often refuse to go to functions or events because they know they will not be able to give their addiction time while they are there**

Early on in their addiction, they will choose to maybe not do it for a while, but they soon learn that the addiction is really in control. They will give in to their addiction when their addiction tells them to.
- **It doesn't matter where they are**
- **It doesn't matter who it will bother**
- **It doesn't matter what it will cost**

the addiction is in charge.

One day, they give up the fight against their addiction – they realize it has won. And very often at that point in their lives:
- **They lose their job**
- **They lose their home**
- **They lose their family**

They lose their will for righteousness.

I am telling you, there is wonderful sweet, refreshing liberty in being surrendered and yielded to God for righteousness.

There is freedom when you,

SURRENDER (commit) YOUR SALVATION TO JESUS CHRIST

2 Timothy 1:10-12 KJV

But is now made manifest by the appearing of our Saviour Jesus Christ, who hath abolished death, and hath brought life and immortality to light through the gospel:

Whereunto I am appointed a preacher, and an apostle, and a teacher of the Gentiles.

For the which cause I also suffer these things: nevertheless I am not ashamed: for I know whom I have believed, and am persuaded that he is able to keep that which I have committed unto him against that day.

I believe a case can be made that the greatest personal battle any of us face is the battle over heaven and hell. Everything in us wants to believe that we are the masters of our own eternity. We don't want to give God authority over that. So we come up with a thousand ways to master eternity:

- **Someone says there is no eternity – we just die and that's it**
- **Someone says there is no heaven and hell – we die and become a part of a greater force**
- **Someone says there is a heaven but no hell – God is too loving to allow anyone to suffer eternally**
- **Someone says heaven is attained by our good works – not by religious affiliation**
- **Someone says heaven is attained by killing anyone whose religion disagrees with theirs**
- **Someone says heaven is attained by joining their church**
- **Someone says heaven is attained by getting baptized**

Mankind has come up with hundreds if not thousands of ways to avoid this one Bible truth; that heaven can only be attained by surrendering our soul's safe keeping to Jesus Christ.

On the eve of his execution for preaching the gospel of Jesus Christ the apostle Paul wrote that whatever happened to him physically, he was not ashamed because He knew the One whom he had committed His soul to and He knew that Christ was (and still is) able to "keep that which he had committed unto him against that day."

Conclusion

There is in the law a very odd provision. The Bible says that every fifty years those who had slaves were supposed to let them go free. But then the Bible makes a provision for those who love their master and choose not to go free. They were to pierce their ear with an awl. Leaving them disfigured and different than everyone else around them. The resulting disfigurement told everyone that this man or woman was a voluntary slave for life.

When you surrender:
* Your will to God's and
  - **Your members to righteousness**
  - **Your salvation to Christ**

It's going to make you different than everyone else around you, except those others who have surrendered the same. Everyone will be able to tell.
  - **Some will think it horrible**
  - **Some will believe it is ugly**
  - **Some will call you a fool**

But you, and the others who have surrendered as you have, will know that the only true freedom comes when we are surrendered to the Lord.

Chapter Nineteen

THE NEW TESTAMENT PRINCIPLE OF LIBERTY
Luke 4:18 (KJV)
The Spirit of the Lord is upon me, because he hath anointed me to preach the gospel to the poor; he hath sent me to heal the brokenhearted, to preach deliverance to the captives, and recovering of sight to the blind, to set at liberty them that are bruised,

Historically, Israel's captivity in Babylon was seventy years long but spiritually, I think an argument can be made that they have not been free ever since. While Daniel was captive God gave him a vision (through Nebuchadnezzar) of the four great Gentile Empires of world history. Daniel and the rest of Israel, were captives of the first two of the four:

- **Babylon**
- **Medo-Persia**

While they were freed to return to their Promised Land under the Medo-Persian Empire,

- **The Grecians under Alexander the Great and Antiochus Epiphanes occupied and ransacked their land**
- **The Romans occupied them after that, eventually crucifying Jesus, destroying Jerusalem, and annihilating those Jews who defied them**

Historically that Roman government eventually collapsed. But

- **Economically**
- **Philosophically**
- **Socially**
- **Legally (as in government)**
- **Spiritually (Roman Catholicism)**

it still exists yet today.

Jesus Christ enters into history during this period of time. Israel was in their Promised Land, but they were not free in the Promised Land.

This chapter marks a shift in our series on liberty…
- **We shift from the Old Testament to the New Testament**
- **We also shift from physical liberty to spiritual liberty**

The passage we are considering is not the first mention of the word liberty in the Bible – even in the New Testament. But as far as the Bible tells us, it is the first time Jesus used the word in His ministry.

Luke 4:18 (KJV)

The Spirit of the Lord is upon me, because he hath anointed me to preach the gospel to the poor; he hath sent me to heal the brokenhearted, to preach deliverance to the captives, and recovering of sight to the blind, to set at liberty them that are bruised,

One of the rules of Hermeneutics (Bible Interpretation) is called "The Law of First Mention". The word liberty is found seventeen times in the New Testament.[1] I am going, for the rest of this book, to approach each of these mentions from the foundation that is laid in Jesus' first mention of liberty.

THE CALL OF CHRIST

Luke 4:14-18 (KJV)

And Jesus returned in the power of the Spirit into Galilee: and there went out a fame of him through all the region round about.
And he taught in their synagogues, being glorified of all.
And he came to Nazareth, where he had been brought up: and, as his custom was, he went into the synagogue on the sabbath day, and stood up for to read.
And there was delivered unto him the book of the prophet Esaias. And when he had opened the book, he found the place where it was written,
The Spirit of the Lord is upon me, because he hath anointed me to preach the gospel to the poor; he hath sent me to heal the

brokenhearted, to preach deliverance to the captives, and recovering of sight to the blind, to set at liberty them that are bruised,

This is Jesus' debut message.
- **Gabriel, the angel had testified that He was *"God with us"*.**
- **John the Baptist has called Him *"the Lamb of God that taketh away the sin of the world"***
- **Andrew, Simon Peter's brother, told Peter, *"we have found the Messias."***

- **He has been called the Lamb**
- **He has been called the Messias**
- **He has been called "God with us"**

But in Christ's first sermon – He opened the Word of God and He here tells us what He came to do.

A. Jesus said He had been anointed to do a particular work

The term anointed means "consecrated to an office." We would much more likely today use the term "called."

I have a calling of God. Being a preacher was in no way my idea. I got saved at the age of 18. By the time I was 21, others were speaking to me about what they thought was God's calling in my life. At the age of 22, I accepted that in fact, God was calling me to serve Him. He had a use for my life that was His own.

When Jesus came, being Himself God, He knew what that anointing, or calling was and He said God had a use for His life that was of God.

B. Jesus said it was the Spirit of the Lord who had anointed Him

So many of our words have a history that seems almost unrelated to what we know the word to mean. Jesus said that the Spirit of the Lord had anointed Him and we know that to mean "chosen or called Him." The word anointing originally meant "to smear or rub with oil."

In the Old Testament the priests were instructed to anoint those items of furniture they would use in the service of the Lord. They would also anoint new priests when they began their life's work. The anointing set them apart. It separated those things strictly for the use that God had for them.

Jesus was set apart from the rest of the World through the Spirit of God in Him. Right from the beginning of His life on this earth
- **He was different**
- **He was unique**
- **He was separated to God**
- **He was anointed for His work**

Even as a child He said to His mother, "I must be about my Father's business."

THE CONCENTRATION OF CHRIST

Luke 4:18
The Spirit of the Lord is upon me, because he hath anointed me to preach the gospel to the poor; he hath sent me to heal the brokenhearted, to preach deliverance to the captives, and recovering of sight to the blind, to set at liberty them that are bruised,

The first time Jesus spoke of liberty He spoke of them that are bruised:
- **Not incarcerated**
- **Not in prison**
- **Not enslaved**

but bruised.

Jesus said He came to, set at liberty them that are bruised.

There are three things I know about bruises:

A. They are the result of some sort of trauma

I don't bruise very often but whenever I have a bruise my wife will see it and ask, "What happened?" If you have a bruise, something happened.

- **You bumped into something**
- **You kicked something**
- **Something fell and hit you**
- **Somebody swung something and hit you**

Jesus came to help bruised and traumatized people.

1. Some of the trauma happens just because we live on this planet.

Not every bad thing that happens, has an explainable reason. Life is just plain hard. We should have figured that out when the very first person who saw us, the one who helped deliver us in this world, turned us upside down and gave us a quick swat on the back side! We didn't do anything wrong We were happily enjoying the comforts of our mothers. Next thing we knew:

- **Pressure started forcing us out of our comfort zone**
- **This nice doctor seemed like he was there to help us until**
- **Suddenly he traumatized us and made us cry**

Life has been that way for us ever since; We've been trying to get comfortable, but pressure keeps pushing us around and next thing we know, we feel like crying.

2. Some of the trauma happens through our own dumb moves

Have you ever done something like this? You get up early in the morning, it's only about half light in the house, and you aren't quite half awake. You shuffle out toward the kitchen to make yourself a cup of coffee and stub your toe on a piece of furniture.

- **You are traumatized**
- **You are in pain**

Your first words are something to the effect of, "Who moved the table here?" Nine times out of ten the table is exactly where it has always been. You just want to blame your pain on someone else.

Our world is training us to think of ourselves as victims. It teaches us to believe we deserve good things and that, if we don't have them, it is someone else's fault.

It's someone else's fault I don't have a good job
- **When it is really because you won't study to have a skill**

It's someone else's fault I don't have good health
- **When it is really because you won't exercise and you eat junk food**

It's someone else's fault I am unhappy
- **When it is really because you choose:**
- **Bad friends**
- **Bad activities**
- **Bad priorities**

3. Some of the trauma happens because we have enemies
We do have enemies in this world. The Bible identifies them as:
- **The world**
- **The flesh**
- **The devil**

Something else I know about bruises,
B. They are internal, not external
If a bruise is on the outside it's not a bruise any more – it's bleeding.

Jesus said,
Matthew 15:17-20 (KJV)

Do not ye yet understand, that whatsoever entereth in at the mouth goeth into the belly, and is cast out into the draught?

But those things which proceed out of the mouth come forth from the heart; and they defile the man.

For out of the heart proceed evil thoughts, murders, adulteries, fornications, thefts, false witness, blasphemies:

These are the things which defile a man: but to eat with unwashen hands defileth not a man.

The deepest problems people face are not those outward ones, but the things that are happening inside. Bruises of the heart, soul and spirit – these are the bruises of the greatest consequence. These are the ones that will most dramatically effect:

- **Your family**
- **Your happiness**
- **Your eternity**

I also know about bruises

C. They show

It is possible physically to bruise your heart or your brain or some other internal organ and for the bruise itself not to be visible. But most of the time when I think of a bruise, It is someplace on my body where I have broken some blood vessels and that blood is visible just under the surface of the skin.

What I mean to say is this; If:

- **Your heart**
- **Your soul**
- **Your spirit**

are in any way traumatized, it's going to result in some outward abnormality. You might think you can hide it – your trauma, your bruise, your brokenness, but it is going to show.

- **It's going to show in how you treat your family**
- **It's going to show in what you think of yourself**

- **It's going to show in how you view life**
- **It's going to show in your relationship with others**

You are bruised, broken and not well. You can deny it and cover it up all you like, but you are the prisoner of your bruises.

That is what Jesus came to set free. If you come to Jesus:
- **He will free your bruised heart and teach you how to truly love**
- **He will free your bruised soul and give you purpose and meaning in life**
- **He will free your bruised spirit and give you life in heaven and fellowship with God**

THE CONCERN OF CHRISTIANITY

The standard of the New Testament is spiritual liberty. Many professing Christians have confused the purpose of faith in Christ to think that Christianity is supposed to free people from the confines of sinful choices.

A. So they believe that Christianity ought to
Promote the new homosexual agenda
After all, these people can't help themselves, they were born this way.

Approve of abortions of babies
After all, we can't expect our young people to restrain their passions until after marriage and to make them raise an unwanted child is unfair to them.

Be gentle to the criminal and thief – and let them out of prison sentences

After all, it is not their fault that they were raised in an environment that wasn't able to develop their inner goodness.

The purpose of the Christian faith is not to be soft on sin. The purpose of Christianity is to show people how to be free from sin

.

B. Nor is Christianity supposed to bea pool of resources for social improvement
Our job isn't to feed the poor and house the homeless. Those are things humans do because it is right to do. Our job isn't to make people's physical lives better. Our job is to point them to eternal life and to urge them to die to self so that they may "set at liberty" the "bruised" that surround them.

Conclusion:
Jesus did not come to open prison doors, although He did that a few times in the Bible. I began to think about it and realized that some of the greatest people in the Bible spent time in prison:
In the Old Testament:
- **Joseph**
- **Jeremiah**
- **Daniel**

In the New Testament:
- **Jesus**
- **Peter**
- **James (was executed)**
- **Paul (multiple times)**
- **Silas**

Some of the freest people I have met are in prison cells. No doubt they suffer, but:

- **Within their cell, they worship and pray and study their Bibles**
- **Within their cell, they witness to others**
- **Within their cell, they faithfully attend every service they can get to**

And sometimes, when they are released, their lives spiritually and emotionally fall apart again.

Also, some of the freest people I know:
- **Live with very little of this world's goods**
- **Live in a body wracked with pain and illness**
- **Live in conditions that are emotionally and physically painful**

But in that pain, they find freedom to rest upon Christ.

The concern and work of Christianity is to set a man free to come to God – whatever their outward conditions might be.

[1] The word is found 18 times in 17 verses.

Chapter Twenty

TOO TRUE

John 8:32-36 (KJV)

And ye shall know the truth, and the truth shall make you free.

They answered him, We be Abraham's seed, and were never in bondage to any man: how sayest thou, Ye shall be made free?

Jesus answered them, Verily, verily, I say unto you, Whosoever committeth sin is the servant of sin.

And the servant abideth not in the house for ever: but the Son abideth ever.

If the Son therefore shall make you free, ye shall be free indeed.

I remember while in school learning about Helen Keller, the little girl who, because of a fever when she was a baby, became blind and deaf. In the early stages of her life Helen Keller was more like a wild animal than a person. She would have fits of anger, wildly swinging her arms and legs in a fashion that was dangerous to herself and those around her. There was no communicating with her. There was only confining her, supervising her and guarding her so that she was safe.

Through a round about connection, Alexander Graham Bell put them in touch with the school where Anne Sullivan had just completed her studies. Sullivan began to work with her when Helen was just seven years old and, through Sullivan, Helen Keller learned to communicate.

In effect, Sullivan set Keller's soul free. She was a thinking, rational, functioning human being, but she was trapped, imprisoned if you will, in a body that would not allow her access to the outside world.

Blindness, as does other forms of handicaps such as lameness and deafness, does that. It imprisons a person so that they are not free to experience all the world that is around them.

There is a kind of blindness that is much less obvious to the observer but
- **It is much more common**
- **It is just as imprisoning**

It is blindness to truth.

It can take a lot of different forms:
A person might be culturally blind –
The Hindi culture, for instance, blinds them so that they cannot see animals as food.
A person might be politically blind –
They cannot see how they can survive without government enablement.
A person might be fiscally blind –
They cannot see how their spending habits are the cause of their financial problems
A person might be socially blind –
They cannot see how rude behavior drives friendships away from them.

I want to address the person who is spiritually blind –
They are therefore unable to see Christ as Saviour, or else to see salvation in its truest light. In many ways a person I think has to feel for the Pharisees and Jews in the time of Christ. These were a people who, for generations, had dedicated themselves to the promise of the Messiah from God.
- **They dreamed of**
- **They looked for**
- **They lived for**
The hope of the coming Messiah – Saviour.

- **It was everything to them**
- **It was their defining distinctive**

They believed God would send to them a Saviour. These people, the Jews, were different than every other people in the world. They were different than the Gentiles to the West of them. They were different than Persians to the East of them or the Egyptians to the south of them. They were different than their cousins, the:
- **Ammonites**
- **Moabites**
- **Edomites**

And the thing that made them different is their faith in a coming Messiah.

So here is Jesus Christ – the Messiah promised by God –
- **They could speak to Him**
- **They could hear His voice**
- **They could see His miracles**

but they couldn't grasp that He was Messiah.

Generations of subtle deterioration, had turned their faith into a religion that, though still claiming to believe in the Messiah, rejected that Messiah could be anyone other than whom they demanded Him to be. They were imprisoned by:
- **Tradition**
- **Expectation**
- **Religion**

But Jesus said the truth would make them free.

THE PERSON OF THE TRUTH

2 John 1:1-2 (KJV)

The elder unto the elect lady and her children, whom I love in the truth; and not I only, but also all they that have known the truth;

For the truth's sake, which dwelleth in us, and shall be with us for ever.

The word truth is used five times in the first four verses of this thirteen-verse letter.

It doesn't take a lot of meditation to see that, by truth, John meant Jesus Christ.

A. He loves these people in the Lord

The only reason he knows these people at all is because of the relationship he and they have with the Lord.

If it had not been for the Lord, John would mostly likely have been fishing with his brother James.

It was Jesus who got him
- **Out of his boat**
- **Away from the sea of Galilee**
- **Into the world, fishing for men**

It was Jesus who had reached into the hearts of this "elect lady" and her children that they had assembled into a local church body.

John, you will remember, was, with his brother James, called "sons of thunder."

They asked Jesus to let them call lightening out of heaven and consume some people they thought were an offense.

Now he says to these people, we will not know until we are in heaven precisely who they are, that he loves them in the truth.

B. He has known the Lord

1 John 1:1 (KJV)

That which was from the beginning, which we have heard, which we have seen with our eyes, which we have looked upon, and our hands have handled, of the Word of life;

The Apostle John has known the Lord through personal:
- **Contact**
- **Communication**

John was one of the three closest to the Lord. From what I can tell:
- **He was there when Jesus was baptized**
- **He was one of the first to be called to follow Him**
- **He witnessed all of Christ's miracles**
- **He leaned on Christ as the last supper**
- **He was with Christ in the garden of Gethsemane**
- **He was there when Jesus was tried**
- **He was there when Jesus was crucified**
- **He was one of the first at the empty tomb**
- **He was one of the first to see the resurrected Saviour**

Then, many others came to know Him through the ministry of John and other witnesses.

I have not seen Christ with my eyes but I know Christ personally.
- **I know how He has changed my life**
- **I have heard His voice through the Word of God**
- **I have witnessed His work in our church and among others**

C. The Lord dwells in us and shall be with us forever

This is true of the Holy Spirit and of the Word of God but is so obviously applied to Christ in this case. This letter is a battle for the truths surrounding Jesus Christ. But more so it is a battle for Christ.
- **It is Christ who is defamed by heresy**
- **It is Christ who is betrayed by backsliders**
- **It is Christ who is trampled by those who lightly treat the faith**

Some people argue that truth is relative. Jesus Christ is not. He is. He is the same yesterday, today, and forever. He is the way the truth and the life for all men.

Christianity is more than a body of doctrines. It is a person
- **Alive**
- **Alert**
- **A coming again**

THE PATH OF THE TRUTH

John 14:6 (KJV)
Jesus saith unto him, I am the way, the truth, and the life: no man cometh unto the Father, but by me.

The truth is a path that leads to the Heavenly Father.

Jesus is taking us somewhere.
- **It's not to a marriage or family life conference**
- **It's not to a motivational or self-improvement talk**
- **It's not to a bigger house of faster car**

Jesus said that His way leads straight to the Father. When I read this, immediately my mind takes me to heaven.

But there are a couple of other steps before we get there. We come to the Father first,
A. For approval
Ephesians 1:6 (KJV)
To the praise of the glory of his grace, wherein he hath made us accepted in the beloved.

It is through Jesus we find reconciliation with God.

- **The anger in the world**
- **The disappointment with ourselves**

- **The distrust of others**

All of that is the result of a broken relationship with God.

We fix our fellowship with God and we fix our relationships with other people.

1 John 4:20 (KJV)
If a man say, I love God, and hateth his brother, he is a liar: for he that loveth not his brother whom he hath seen, how can he love God whom he hath not seen?

When we fix our relationship with God we even fix our issues with ourself.
1 John 3:19 (KJV)
And hereby we know that we are of the truth, and shall assure our hearts before him.

Did you know that every chapter of First John says something about our relationships with people? First John is a test for true salvation. So closely tied is our relationship with people to our relationship with God that, one cannot be effected without the other.

We come to the Father for approval

Then we come to the Father,
B. For answers
1 John 5:14-15 (KJV)
And this is the confidence that we have in him, that, if we ask any thing according to his will, he heareth us:
And if we know that he hear us, whatsoever we ask, we know that we have the petitions that we desired of him.

The subject of prayer is such an obviously spiritual thing that it might almost seem unnecessary to speak on it. Except it is also so often instructed upon in the Word of God. Just in the Gospels we have:

The Lord's Model Prayer
Matthew 6:9-14 (KJV)
...Our Father which art in heaven, Hallowed be thy name.
Thy kingdom come. Thy will be done in earth, as it is in heaven.
Give us this day our daily bread.
And forgive us our debts, as we forgive our debtors.
And lead us not into temptation, but deliver us from evil: For thine is the kingdom, and the power, and the glory, for ever. Amen.
For if ye forgive men their trespasses, your heavenly Father will also forgive you:

The Lord's Promise of Prayer
Matthew 7:7-11 (KJV)
Ask, and it shall be given you; seek, and ye shall find; knock, and it shall be opened unto you:
For every one that asketh receiveth; and he that seeketh findeth; and to him that knocketh it shall be opened.
Or what man is there of you, whom if his son ask bread, will he give him a stone?
Or if he ask a fish, will he give him a serpent?
If ye then, being evil, know how to give good gifts unto your children, how much more shall your Father which is in heaven give good things to them that ask him?

The Lord's Example of Prayer
John 17:1 (KJV)
These words spake Jesus, and lifted up his eyes to heaven, and said, Father, the hour is come; glorify thy Son, that thy Son also may glorify thee:

Then we have this condemnation,
James 4:1-3 (KJV)
From whence come wars and fightings among you? come they not hence, even of your lusts that war in your members?

Ye lust, and have not: ye kill, and desire to have, and cannot obtain: ye fight and war, yet ye have not, because ye ask not.
Ye ask, and receive not, because ye ask amiss, that ye may consume it upon your lusts.

But Jesus is our path to access the Father. In Him we have answers. We come to the Father for approval and then we come to the Father for answers, and in the end…

We come to the Father,
C. For all time
John 14:2-3 (KJV)
In my Father's house are many mansions: if it were not so, I would have told you. I go to prepare a place for you.
And if I go and prepare a place for you, I will come again, and receive you unto myself; that where I am, there ye may be also.

THE PROMISE OF THE TRUTH

John 8:32 (KJV)
And ye shall know the truth, and the truth shall make you free.

John 8:36 (KJV)
If the Son therefore shall make you free, ye shall be free indeed.

By comparing these verses we have another verification that the Person of truth is Jesus Christ.

The promise of truth is freedom. But even those Jews who believed on Him did not understand. John 8:31-32 (KJV)
Then said Jesus to those Jews which believed on him, If ye continue in my word, then are ye my disciples indeed;
And ye shall know the truth, and the truth shall make you free.

Jesus told them that if they continued in His Word they would be free. Their response was, "We've never been in bondage!"

To which Jesus responded, "*…Whosoever committeth sin is the servant of sin.*"

To know Jesus, and to continue in His word provides:
A. Freedom from the wages of sin
Romans 6:23 (KJV)
For the wages of sin is death; but the gift of God is eternal life through Jesus Christ our Lord.

This is salvation. I do not dread eternity.

B. Freedom from the guilt of sin
1 Timothy 1:12-15 (KJV)
And I thank Christ Jesus our Lord, who hath enabled me, for that he counted me faithful, putting me into the ministry;
Who was before a blasphemer, and a persecutor, and injurious: but I obtained mercy, because I did it ignorantly in unbelief.
And the grace of our Lord was exceeding abundant with faith and love which is in Christ Jesus.
This is a faithful saying, and worthy of all acceptation, that Christ Jesus came into the world to save sinners; of whom I am chief.

This is satisfaction. Paul never forgot that he was a sinner. But he never let that hold him down from serving Jesus.

C. Freedom from the power of sin
Romans 6:14 (KJV)
For sin shall not have dominion over you: for ye are not under the law, but under grace.

This is sanctification. From the moment we get saved, we have the power to dominate the sin nature. We don't overcome all of our sin in a day or even in a lifetime. As we trust Christ and continue learning and applying his Word, one by one, we get victory.

Conclusion

John 8:32 (KJV)

And ye shall know the truth, and the truth shall make you free.

What a tragedy to be so close to liberty, but to miss it because you can't even see that you are a prisoner. What a shame it would be to leave today, looking freedom in the face, but to miss it because you are blinded and trapped

- **Culturally**
- **Socially**
- **Spiritually**

and do not come to Jesus Christ

Chapter Twenty-One

LIBERTY OF THE SOUL

Acts 22:3-28 (KJV)

I am verily a man which am a Jew, born in Tarsus, a city in Cilicia, yet brought up in this city at the feet of Gamaliel, and taught according to the perfect manner of the law of the fathers, and was zealous toward God, as ye all are this day.

And I persecuted this way unto the death, binding and delivering into prisons both men and women.

As also the high priest doth bear me witness, and all the estate of the elders: from whom also I received letters unto the brethren, and went to Damascus, to bring them which were there bound unto Jerusalem, for to be punished.

And it came to pass, that, as I made my journey, and was come nigh unto Damascus about noon, suddenly there shone from heaven a great light round about me.

And I fell unto the ground, and heard a voice saying unto me, Saul, Saul, why persecutest thou me?

And I answered, Who art thou, Lord? And he said unto me, I am Jesus of Nazareth, whom thou persecutest.

And they that were with me saw indeed the light, and were afraid; but they heard not the voice of him that spake to me.

And I said, What shall I do, Lord? And the Lord said unto me, Arise, and go into Damascus; and there it shall be told thee of all things which are appointed for thee to do.

And when I could not see for the glory of that light, being led by the hand of them that were with me, I came into Damascus.

And one Ananias, a devout man according to the law, having a good report of all the Jews which dwelt there,

Came unto me, and stood, and said unto me, Brother Saul, receive thy sight. And the same hour I looked up upon him.

And he said, The God of our fathers hath chosen thee, that thou shouldest know his will, and see that Just One, and shouldest hear the voice of his mouth.

For thou shalt be his witness unto all men of what thou hast seen and heard.

And now why tarriest thou? arise, and be baptized, and wash away thy sins, calling on the name of the Lord.

And it came to pass, that, when I was come again to Jerusalem, even while I prayed in the temple, I was in a trance;

And saw him saying unto me, Make haste, and get thee quickly out of Jerusalem: for they will not receive thy testimony concerning me.

And I said, Lord, they know that I imprisoned and beat in every synagogue them that believed on thee:

And when the blood of thy martyr Stephen was shed, I also was standing by, and consenting unto his death, and kept the raiment of them that slew him.

And he said unto me, Depart: for I will send thee far hence unto the Gentiles.

And they gave him audience unto this word, and then lifted up their voices, and said, Away with such a fellow from the earth: for it is not fit that he should live.

And as they cried out, and cast off their clothes, and threw dust into the air,

The chief captain commanded him to be brought into the castle, and bade that he should be examined by scourging; that he might know wherefore they cried so against him.

And as they bound him with thongs, Paul said unto the centurion that stood by, Is it lawful for you to scourge a man that is a Roman, and uncondemned?

When the centurion heard that, he went and told the chief captain, saying, Take heed what thou doest: for this man is a Roman.

Then the chief captain came, and said unto him, Tell me, art thou a Roman? He said, Yea.

And the chief captain answered, With a great sum obtained I this freedom. And Paul said, But I was free born.

Many of you might remember that I ended last week's message by claiming that many of the greatest characters of the Bible spent time in prison. In the Old Testament:

- **Joseph**
- **Jeremiah**
- **Daniel**

In the New Testament:

- **Jesus**
- **Peter**
- **James (was executed)**

- **John**
- **Paul (multiple times)**
- **Silas**

The Apostle Paul is the most notable of those characters, especially in the New Testament. Did you realize that 25% of the book of Acts is a chronicle of Paul in prison Then consider that a significant portion of the New Testament was written by him while he was in prison.

- **Paul wrote half of the New Testament**
- **He wrote half of that as a prisoner**

Every Bible believer Christian is a:

- **Fan of a felon**
- **Devotee of a detainee**
- **Booster of a bandit**
- **Disciple of a desperado**
- **Groupie of a gangster**

We have every reason to be humble and motive to be merciful to those whose choices up until now have left them captive.

Paul made frequent reference to his being a prisoner and, while he never gloried in it, he also never hid that he had been a wicked man before his salvation. A full one-quarter of the book of Acts is a chronicle of Paul's capture and imprisonment by the Romans at the behest of the Jews. Yet in these eight chapters[1] the word liberty is used in connection with Paul three times and the word freedom is used once.

Paul had what I am going to call here,

LIBERTY OF MINISTRY

Acts 24:23 (KJV)
And he commanded a centurion to keep Paul, and to let him have liberty, and that he should forbid none of his acquaintance to minister or come unto him.

In order to show the full content of my thought here I need to jump a few chapters further into the Book of Acts and look at: Acts 28:16-21 (KJV)

And when we came to Rome, the centurion delivered the prisoners to the captain of the guard: but Paul was suffered to dwell by himself with a soldier that kept him.

And it came to pass, that after three days Paul called the chief of the Jews together: and when they were come together, he said unto them, Men and brethren, though I have committed nothing against the people, or customs of our fathers, yet was I delivered prisoner from Jerusalem into the hands of the Romans.

Who, when they had examined me, would have let me go, because there was no cause of death in me.

But when the Jews spake against it, I was constrained to appeal unto Caesar; not that I had ought to accuse my nation of.

For this cause therefore have I called for you, to see you, and to speak with you: …

- **In chapter 24 Paul is free to be ministered to**
- **In chapter 28 Paul is free to minister or to preach**

In both cases he was a prisoner of Rome. The Caesar would soon sentence him to death, and even if he had let him go free, the Jews would surely have assassinated him. He is in this world,

- **Hated**
- **Hounded**
- **Harangued**

Still he is at liberty to preach the Word of God.

- **To minister and be ministered to**
- **To bless and to be blessed**

No matter what your outward circumstances are you are, always free to preach the Word of God and to attend preaching of the Word of God. There have been times in history when those who have preached have been:

- **Harassed**
- **Fined**
- **Imprisoned**
- **Killed**

for preaching. But they preached until their dying breath.

Believers have at times been forced to:
- **Assemble for services far out in the woods**
- **Hide their congregations in barns or behind butchers meat**
- **Gather near a prison window to hear their pastor's message**

But the fact is, you have a God given liberty to both hear the Word of God and to preach the Word of God, if you are inclined to do so.

History is filled with accounts of those who hate Christians attempting to:
- **Defeat them**
- **Defile them**
- **Delete them**

Their 2000 years of failure, despite the fact that they have always:
- **Outnumbered**
- **Out financed**
- **Out powered**

the Christians, proves that you and I are free to preach and to be preached to – regardless of the trying of the world – if we want to be preached to and if we have a heart to preach.

I see what I will call Paul's

LIBERTY OF FELLOWSHIP

Acts 27:3 (KJV)
And the next day we touched at Sidon. And Julius courteously entreated Paul, and gave him liberty to go unto his friends to refresh himself.

This passage sounds a lot like the first one in Acts 24 but this one does not use the word minister. I am going to take advantage of that to speak about the difference between the "preaching/teaching" aspects of church life and the "fellowship" aspects.

There is a relationship that Christians have outside of church, and I recognize that the context sounds like something other than an official church service, but I'm pretty sure that we ought to view this as Christian gathering in a meaningful way.

A. It was with friends not a friend
Just "gonna" be honest – it's a lot easier to get into a wrong spirited gossip type conversation with one person than it is with a group. I am not fond of the "best friend" mentality anyway. As Christians we ought to practice what Paul did and be "all things to all men that we might by all means save some" When we get into a best friend idea – we stop trying to reach out to others and we start trying to cultivate the one friendship. When you put together a group of Christians you almost have to have some sense of organization to it.

I think this is an organized fellowship.
B. It was to refresh himself
Word refresh here is a derivative of a couple of words that, taken together mean, "prepared hospitality."

When I pastored in Astoria, OR we had a Filipino family in our church. One day, just after we first met them, they invited my family to have a meal. When we got there we found that it wasn't a meal, it was a feast. There was every kind of Pilipino treat imaginable – the only one I can remember by name is Lumpia, but it was unbelievable. I found out later the lady of the house had all her sisters and cousins and nieces cooking for days to prepare that one dinner.

Believe me – it was refreshing.

There is then what I am going to call Paul's,

LIBERTY OF CONSEQUENCE

Acts 26:32 (KJV)

Then said Agrippa unto Festus, This man might have been set at liberty, if he had not appealed unto Caesar.

This verse might seem to you to be irrelevant to your personal life. But I promise you, you argue the point of the passage in your head almost every day.

Festus and Agrippa agreed here that, had Paul not appealed to Caesar, they could have let him go. Remember what Paul had gone through up until this point.

- **He had been assaulted at the Temple in Jerusalem – the Jews were going to beat him to death on the spot**
- **He had been "rescued" by the Romans guards, but only narrowly escaped being beaten by them until he confessed to some reason for being close to killed by the Jews**
- **He had been sneaked out of Jerusalem to Caesarea Philippi because there were people in Jerusalem who had sworn an oath not to eat or drink anything until they had killed Paul**
- **He had been kept in prison in Caesarea Philippi for two years while Felix tried to extract a bribe from him and his friends**
- **He had been falsely accused by Jewish leaders who had one time been his friends and colleagues**

The Romans didn't really know what to do with him. They didn't think he was guilty of anything that should keep him in prison or have him to be killed. But then, they were there to try to keep the Jews happy as best they could. They suggested that Paul go back to Jerusalem to be tried by a court system that would better understand the nature of the accusations against

Paul. He knew that would have meant a mock trial and execution so he appealed to go to Rome instead.

Now all of a sudden, they are telling him that if he had not appealed to Caesar, they would just let him go. He's in a "no win" situation. The question is, "Where is God then?" There isn't a good choice to make – whatever you do – someone is going to get hurt, and it looks like it's going to be you. How do you obey God then? What about 1 Corinthians 10:13 (KJV)
There hath no temptation taken you but such as is common to man: but God is faithful, who will not suffer you to be tempted above that ye are able; but will with the temptation also make a way to escape, that ye may be able to bear it.

- **Where is Paul's way of escape? More to the point…**
- **Where is my way of escape?**

A. Paul knew before he went to Jerusalem that bonds and imprisonment awaited him there

Acts 21:10-12 (KJV)
And as we tarried there many days, there came down from Judaea a certain prophet, named Agabus.
And when he was come unto us, he took Paul's girdle, and bound his own hands and feet, and said, Thus saith the Holy Ghost, So shall the Jews at Jerusalem bind the man that owneth this girdle, and shall deliver him into the hands of the Gentiles.
And when we heard these things, both we, and they of that place, besought him not to go up to Jerusalem.

He went to Jerusalem aware of the consequences. I would suggest that, way before we ever get to that place where there is no good choice; we have been warned that we are heading to a place where there is no good choice.

B. Paul was willing to suffer for the sake of the Gospel

Acts 21:13 (KJV)

Then Paul answered, What mean ye to weep and to break mine heart? for I am ready not to be bound only, but also to die at Jerusalem for the name of the Lord Jesus.

I am reminded of the missionary Jim Elliot. He and four other missionaries were all murdered by a tribe of natives in Ecuador well known to be murderous. They did what they could to reduce their risks. But they were all willing to accept the consequences of trying to give the gospel to these natives.

My suggestion to you is that, if you are not willing to accept the negative consequences for a certain path you are on, change course before you find yourself in a spot where there is no good choice.

C. Paul wrote about half of the New Testament while he was a prisoner

That tells me that good things can still happen in bad circumstances. Maybe you find yourself in a place in life where there just isn't any good choice. Choose to do good right there.

Conclusion

Paul was a "free prisoner". That's a good way to view yourself. If you are a Christian, the circumstances of life can confine you all they will – you are free because "where the Spirit of the Lord is," no matter what else may or may not be there, "there is liberty."

[1] Acts chapters 21-18

Chapter Twenty-Two

GLORIOUS LIBERTY

Romans 8:21

When I think of freedom and liberty, I think of them in such glowing terms already that there are very few adjectives that serve to enhance it.

Who would ever say:
- **Really good liberty**
- **Wonderful liberty**
- **Great liberty**
- **Nice liberty**
- **Huge liberty**

Maybe a person could say something like, "Oh marvelous liberty!" But really – the liberty is marvelous enough on its own. It almost needs no further description.

That's why, what I found in Romans 8:21, that God refers to the liberty of the children of God as "glorious liberty" it got my attention.

THE GLORIOUS NEWS

Romans 8:1 (KJV)
There is therefore now no condemnation to them which are in Christ Jesus, who walk not after the flesh, but after the Spirit.

Those of you who are saved, can you remember what it was living under the condemnation of your sin? I got saved as a fairly young adult, but I had not been a great guy before I got saved. I had done things so wrong, sinful, so opposed to God that I lived in constant guilt. Even after I got saved, I lived in terror of going to heaven and having God show some big screen replay of my sins for all to see.

So when I saw this verse my soul was quite literally set free,
- **There is no condemnation**
- **There is no memory**
- **There is no replay in heaven of all my sins**

There is no condemnation.
- **There is no condemnation before God**
- **There is no condemnation before the other believers**
- **There is therefore no need to condemn myself**

THE GLORIOUS LIBERATOR

Romans 8:2 (KJV)
For the law of the Spirit of life in Christ Jesus hath made me free from the law of sin and death.

The glory in this verse is in the fact that I do not have to set myself free.

I am thinking about the prisoner of war in a Rambo movie. He can't set himself free. He can't fight his way out of the enemy camp:
- **He is bruised and starving**
- **He is weak and wounded**
- **He is vulnerable and without weapons**

He needs a rescuer.
- **Someone who is strong and rested and healthy and armed to the teeth with weapons**
- **Someone who knows the enemy's whereabouts and has plans for every contingency**
- **Someone who is so much better at what he does than our captors and shows no mercy when they put up a fight against him**

That's Christ Jesus and the law of the Spirit of life. It's no contest. When Jesus comes to set us free, our enemy might as well run away – he doesn't stand a chance.

THE GLORIOUS CONQUEST

Romans 8:3 (KJV)
For what the law could not do, in that it was weak through the flesh, God sending his own Son in the likeness of sinful flesh, and for sin, condemned sin in the flesh:

Notice the "reversal of fortune" in this text:
- **In verse one I was concerned about being condemned for my sin**
- **In verse 3 it is my sin that is condemned**

The condemnation is so far removed that I can:
- **Never lose my salvation**
- **Never lose my seat in heavenly places**
- **Never lose my relationship with my Heavenly Father**

THE GLORIOUS RESULTS

Having been made free, the remainder of Romans chapter eight lists at least eight results or benefits of our glorious liberty:

A. The law fulfilled

Romans 8:4 (KJV)
That the righteousness of the law might be fulfilled in us, who walk not after the flesh, but after the Spirit.

James said that *"if we keep the whole law, and yet offend in one point, we are guilty of it all."*[1]

Because of Jesus Christ, we have already fulfilled the whole law.

B. The Lord is pleased

Romans 8:7-9 (KJV)

Because the carnal mind is enmity against God: for it is not subject to the law of God, neither indeed can be.

So then they that are in the flesh cannot please God.

But ye are not in the flesh, but in the Spirit, if so be that the Spirit of God dwell in you. Now if any man have not the Spirit of Christ, he is none of his.

Before I was saved, I could not please God and very often did not try to please God. Because when God looks at me, He sees Jesus Christ, I cannot help but please God.

C. The spirit is alive

Romans 8:10-11 (KJV)

And if Christ be in you, the body is dead because of sin; but the Spirit is life because of righteousness.

But if the Spirit of him that raised up Jesus from the dead dwell in you, he that raised up Christ from the dead shall also quicken your mortal bodies by his Spirit that dwelleth in you.

Paul said that the man who is not saved is *"dead in trespasses and sins."* But because of Jesus Christ my spirit has been quickened to life again. That means I can fellowship with God, my Heavenly Father.

D. The inheritance is ours

Romans 8:14-17 (KJV)

For as many as are led by the Spirit of God, they are the sons of God.

For ye have not received the spirit of bondage again to fear; but ye have received the Spirit of adoption, whereby we cry, Abba, Father.

The Spirit itself beareth witness with our spirit, that we are the children of God:

And if children, then heirs; heirs of God, and joint-heirs with Christ; if so be that we suffer with him, that we may be also glorified together.

Before I was saved the wrath of God abode upon me. But because of Jesus Christ, I am a joint heir with Him and have an inheritance awaiting me.

E. The expectation is deliverance

Romans 8:18-24 (KJV)

For I reckon that the sufferings of this present time are not worthy to be compared with the glory which shall be revealed in us.

For the earnest expectation of the creature waiteth for the manifestation of the sons of God.

For the creature was made subject to vanity, not willingly, but by reason of him who hath subjected the same in hope,

Because the creature itself also shall be delivered from the bondage of corruption into the glorious liberty of the children of God.

For we know that the whole creation groaneth and travaileth in pain together until now.

And not only they, but ourselves also, which have the firstfruits of the Spirit, even we ourselves groan within ourselves, waiting for the adoption, to wit, the redemption of our body.

For we are saved by hope: but hope that is seen is not hope: for what a man seeth, why doth he yet hope for?

Before I got saved I had no hope in this world. I would just have lived as well as I could and hoped for the best after death. But because of Jesus Christ I have a hope that is sure, promised and guaranteed.

- **I am saved**
- **I have a home in heaven**
- **I have an eternity that is bright**

No doubt about it. I need never question it.

F. The Spirit is our helper

Romans 8:26-27 (KJV)

Likewise the Spirit also helpeth our infirmities: for we know not what we should pray for as we ought: but the Spirit itself maketh intercession for us with groanings which cannot be uttered.
And he that searcheth the hearts knoweth what is the mind of the Spirit, because he maketh intercession for the saints according to the will of God.

I prayed before I was saved, but I never knew if my prayers got answered. But because of Jesus Christ I have a helper in times of need. The Holy Spirit guides my prayers through the Bible and He prays Himself when I can't seem to phrase the right words. Because of Jesus Christ I can be confident that, when I ask anything in His name he hears and He answers.

G. The purpose of God is good
Romans 8:28-30 (KJV)
And we know that all things work together for good to them that love God, to them who are the called according to his purpose.
For whom he did foreknow, he also did predestinate to be conformed to the image of his Son, that he might be the firstborn among many brethren.
Moreover whom he did predestinate, them he also called: and whom he called, them he also justified: and whom he justified, them he also glorified.

Not everything that happens in life is good. But because of Jesus Christ I can rest in this promise that everything will work together for good.

H. Nothing shall separate us
Romans 8:31-39 (KJV)
What shall we then say to these things? If God be for us, who can be against us?
He that spared not his own Son, but delivered him up for us all, how shall he not with him also freely give us all things?
Who shall lay anything to the charge of God's elect? It is God that justifieth.

Who is he that condemneth? It is Christ that died, yea rather, that is risen again, who is even at the right hand of God, who also maketh intercession for us.
Who shall separate us from the love of Christ? shall tribulation, or distress, or persecution, or famine, or nakedness, or peril, or sword?
As it is written, For thy sake we are killed all the day long; we are accounted as sheep for the slaughter.
Nay, in all these things we are more than conquerors through him that loved us.
For I am persuaded, that neither death, nor life, nor angels, nor principalities, nor powers, nor things present, nor things to come,
Nor height, nor depth, nor any other creature, shall be able to separate us from the love of God, which is in Christ Jesus our Lord.

Because of Jesus Christ, nothing is able to separate me from the love of God

- **Not death**
- **Not life**
- **Not angels**
- **Not principalities**
- **Not powers**
- **Not things present**
- **Not things to come**
- **Not height**
- **Not depth**
- **Not any other creature**

I am free. I am at liberty. And it is glorious liberty.

[1] James 2:10 (KJV)
For whosoever shall keep the whole law, and yet offend in one point, he is guilty of all.

Chapter Twenty-Three

USE YOUR FREEDOM

1 Corinthians 7:17-23 (KJV)

But as God hath distributed to every man, as the Lord hath called every one, so let him walk. And so ordain I in all churches.

Is any man called being circumcised? let him not become uncircumcised. Is any called in uncircumcision? let him not be circumcised.

Circumcision is nothing, and uncircumcision is nothing, but the keeping of the commandments of God.

Let every man abide in the same calling wherein he was called.

Art thou called being a servant? care not for it: but if thou mayest be made free, use it rather.

For he that is called in the Lord, being a servant, is the Lord's freeman: likewise also he that is called, being free, is Christ's servant.

Ye are bought with a price; be not ye the servants of men.

We are looking at perhaps one of the most controversial passages in the New Testament. It is without question one of the most controversial of 1 Corinthians; a controversial book in and of itself. It would not be impossible for any of us to focus so much on the things that are on the surface that we miss may of the weightier lessons that run just under the surface. You will find both words in the chapter:

1 Corinthians 7:21

Art thou called being a servant? care not for it: but if thou mayest be made free, use it rather.

1 Corinthians 7:39 (KJV)

The wife is bound by the law as long as her husband liveth; but if her husband be dead, she is at liberty to be married to whom she will; only in the Lord.

But then there are plenty of other words found in the chapter that relate to liberty – or the lack thereof:

1 Corinthians 7:4 (KJV)

The wife hath not power of her own body, but the husband: and likewise also the husband hath not power of his own body, but the wife.

1 Corinthians 7:15 (KJV)
But if the unbelieving depart, let him depart. A brother or a sister is not under bondage in such cases: but God hath called us to peace.

1 Corinthians 7:27 (KJV)
Art thou bound unto a wife? seek not to be loosed. Art thou loosed from a wife? seek not a wife.

1 Corinthians 7:39 (KJV)
The wife is bound by the law as long as her husband liveth; but if her husband be dead, she is at liberty to be married to whom she will; only in the Lord.

CONTEXT

1 Corinthians 7:1 (KJV)
Now concerning the things whereof ye wrote unto me: It is good for a man not to touch a woman.

Most fundamental type Bible students believe that this section of the letter is Paul's response to some questions asked of him by the members of the church there in Corinth. We tend to interpret Paul's answers to those questions based more on the times in which we live rather than the times in which they lived.

To get the best sense of the chapter we have to "put ourselves in their shoes." These are people who could very easily be killed for their faith in Christ. The threat to their lives was very real and absolutely imminent. It could happen at any time:
- **A neighbor reports you to the authorities**
- **Soldiers surround your house and break the door in**
- **You are dragged to a pit or dungeon**

- **After torture and attempts, to get you to renounce Christ**
- **You would be killed in the most horrific of ways**

A very sincere question then is; "Should we really marry and bring children into this environment?"

Now, I know how I was as a young man, almost forty years ago; and I don't think young men have changed that much since I was a young man, almost forty years ago. I graduated from High School, moved out into my own place and realized immediately that I was lonely. And I decided that my number one priority after graduating High School needed to be to get married. God did not let me do that – although I tried very hard to make it happen,

I have to tell you, I was not thinking very level headed back then:
- **I wasn't thinking about how I would support a wife, if I got one**
- **I wasn't thinking about how I would pay for children, if we had them**
- **I wasn't thinking about anyone but myself**

I was lonely and I wanted to fix it.

- **I know a bunch of guys who were not thinking when they got married**
- **And I know a bunch of gals who married them when they weren't thinking**

And it caused a wreck in their lives. Sometimes they wrecked kids along the way.

This chapter is an attempt on the part of the Christians of that era to think before marriage.
- **What if a man got married and then was dragged away to be executed for his faith?**
- **How would his wife be cared for?**

- **What if a husband and wife had children and the two of them were captured and killed?**
- **Who would raise his children?**

You see, they were not living in a "grab all you can and can all you get" world. Life was a serious thing.

So the questions are these:
- **Should a person marry at all in these very dangerous days?**
- **Should a father give away his daughter to marriage?**
- **Should a widow or widower get married again?**

And then there is the question,

D. "What if I am a believer and my spouse is not?"

Every one of these questions is:
- **Legitimate**
- **Sincere**
- **Urgent**

in their world.

But they are also being asked to a man they knew had personally never gotten married.

Paul's answers are as follows:
- **It's better to marry than to commit immorality**
- **It's better to be free to serve the Lord than to marry**
- **It's better not to marry than to marry someone who is not a Christian**
- **It's better to commit to one spouse for the rest of their lives, even if they do leave you**

The person who marries is bound by the law of Christ to their spouse until that spouse dies. Marriage should never, ever, be entered into lightly.

But I would like to move us from here to what I am going to call an,

UNDERLYING LESSON

1 Corinthians 7:6 (KJV)
But I speak this by permission, and not of commandment.

1 Corinthians 7:10 (KJV)
And unto the married I command, yet not I, but the Lord, Let not the wife depart from her husband:

1 Corinthians 7:12 (KJV)
But to the rest speak I, not the Lord: If any brother hath a wife that believeth not, and she be pleased to dwell with him, let him not put her away.

1 Corinthians 7:25 (KJV)
Now concerning virgins I have no commandment of the Lord: yet I give my judgment, as one that hath obtained mercy of the Lord to be faithful.

1 Corinthians 7:40 (KJV)
But she is happier if she so abide, after my judgment: and I think also that I have the Spirit of God.

With the exception of one place in this chapter, Paul very clearly says that his answers in this chapter:
- **Are not commandments**
- **Are his judgment rather than the Lord's**

I have a question for you; "Does that mean we can ignore the bulk of this chapter?" Since Paul said that these answers were his opinions, that they were from him and not the Lord, does that mean a man and a woman can live together outside of marriage without disobeying the Bible? Does it mean that this chapter is less inspired and less the Word of God than other parts of the Bible?

I would suggest to you that there are two phrases in this chapter that indicate that this chapter is just as God breathed, just as inspired and just as much the Word of God as is John 3:16. Toward the beginning of the chapter,
1 Corinthians 7:6 (KJV)
But I speak this by permission, and not of commandment.

At the end of the chapter,
1 Corinthians 7:40 (KJV)
But she is happier if she so abide, after my judgment: and I think also that I have the Spirit of God.

The chapter is framed by two phrases:
- **Number one, I have permission to say this**
- **Number two, I think I have the Spirit of God**

Even though Paul, at the moment of the writing of this chapter, could not attest that what he wrote here was "the Word of the Lord." The intrinsic evidence, the clues God left us in the chapter itself, give us every confidence that it is the Word of God.
- **He teaches truths that are corroborated in other places in the Bible[1]**
- **He uses arguments that are clearly inspired in other portions of the Bible[2]**
- **He upholds a principle that is upheld throughout the Bible[3]**

I think it is important for me to bring this up today to show that, *"All Scripture is given by inspiration of God, and is profitable..."*[4] even if the man of God who delivered it did not know it was Scripture when he delivered it. And to demonstrate that a man of God does not have to know that God is at work in his work to be uniquely blessed of God.

One of the arguments of those who believe it is ok to use any version of the Bible we want to use will invariably be, "The translators of the King James Bible never claimed that the King James was perfect." Two things:

- **First, can you imagine that cries of arrogance they would have heard (would still be hearing) if they had claimed perfection?**
- **Second, that their work was perfect was not theirs to claim as much as it is God's to prove**

I would insist God has proven it to be the perfect and infallible Word of God:

- **By the change it has seen in the world**
- **By the fact that no Bible after it was translated from the same source**
- **By the opposition Satan has mounted against it**

APPLICATION

1 Corinthians 7:21 (KJV)
Art thou called being a servant? care not for it: but if thou mayest be made free, use it rather.

I believe the entire chapter is meant to bring us to this spiritual application and truth: be free and use your freedom. If Christ has made you free in any capacity, use your freedom for Christ and:

A. The gospel

2 Corinthians 4:3 (KJV)
But if our gospel be hid, it is hid to them that are lost:

There is a sentiment in this verses that ought to grab the heart of the Christian; the gospel can be hidden.

- **It is the lost person who can't see it**
- **It is the devil who is behind it**
- **It is the Christian who has to uncover it**

- **You are free in that you are saved**
- **You are free in that you have time**
- **You are free in that you have the means**

Use that freedom to uncover the gospel.

Use your freedom for Christ and
B. Spiritual growth
2 Peter 3:18 (KJV)
But grow in grace, and in the knowledge of our Lord and Saviour Jesus Christ. To him be glory both now and for ever. Amen.

- **Don't be a Christian wallflower**
- **Don't be a Christian bench warmer**
- **Don't be a Christian with stunted growth**

- **Grow in grace and in the knowledge of our Lord and Saviour Jesus Christ**
- **Press toward the mark for the prize of the high calling of God in Christ Jesus**
- **Run your Christian race to obtain the crown**

- **Get stirred up**
- **Get fired up**
- **Get up**

and grow as a believer.

Use your freedom for Christ and
C. The world
Romans 1:9-12 (KJV)
For God is my witness, whom I serve with my spirit in the gospel of his Son, that without ceasing I make mention of you always in my prayers; Making request, if by any means now at length I might have a prosperous journey by the will of God to come unto you.
For I long to see you, that I may impart unto you some spiritual gift, to the end ye may be established; That is, that I may be comforted together with you by the mutual faith both of you and me.

Paul told the Romans that, though he had never met them, he wanted to come see them so that they could be a blessing to each other.

- **He wanted to be a blessing to them**
- **He knew they could also be a blessing to him**

And I just want to say, don't let yourself get stuck in your world.

There are others that you can be a blessing to:

- **Someone that you work with**
- **Someone that you see at the store or the filling station**
- **Someone who is going to open the envelope with the bill you've paid**
- **Someone who sits alone in a nursing home**

You can be a blessing to them.

And you will discover that they will be a blessing to you too.

Conclusion

It would be very difficult for any of us in the United States to argue we are not free. It may be that we lose those freedoms very soon. Right now, today, we are free. Use your freedom for Jesus Christ.

[1] Jesus taught us not to lust after a woman, Paul said we should not burn after her.
[2] Romans 7 also says that those that are married are bound in marriage until the spouse dies.
[3] That a man should be "free indeed."
[4] 2 Timothy 3:16

Chapter Twenty-Four

NO TRIPPING HERE

1 Corinthians 8:4-9 (KJV)

As concerning therefore the eating of those things that are offered in sacrifice unto idols, we know that an idol is nothing in the world, and that there is none other God but one.

For though there be that are called gods, whether in heaven or in earth, (as there be gods many, and lords many,)

But to us there is but one God, the Father, of whom are all things, and we in him; and one Lord Jesus Christ, by whom are all things, and we by him.

Howbeit there is not in every man that knowledge: for some with conscience of the idol unto this hour eat it as a thing offered unto an idol; and their conscience being weak is defiled.

But meat commendeth us not to God: for neither, if we eat, are we the better; neither, if we eat not, are we the worse.

But take heed lest by any means this liberty of your;s become a stumblingblock to them that are weak.

2 Corinthians 3:17 (KJV) says,

Now the Lord is that Spirit: and where the Spirit of the Lord is, there is liberty.

I am grateful for that liberty, aren't you?

- **We are free to live for Jesus Christ**
- **We are free from the judgment of sin**
- **We are free from the fear of eternal hell**
- **We are free from trying to earn our way into heaven**

But the passage we have before us tells us that we must exercise some caution with our liberty. We don't want our liberty to be a stumblingblock for someone that is weak. Stumblingblocks in themselves are not always bad things.

This weakness does not necessarily mean a weak Christian. It can also refer to a man or woman who is weak by reason of their lost position.

JESUS IS A STUMBLING STONE

Romans 9:33 (KJV)
As it is written, Behold, I lay in Sion a stumblingstone and rock of offence: and whosoever believeth on him shall not be ashamed.

The passage is an obvious reference to the Lord Jesus Christ and I notice several things from the verse:
This stumblingstone was,

A. Laid by God

Let's just go ahead and admit that there are some things that God can do with righteousness that we cannot.

- **God can be jealous righteously**
- **God can exercise vengeance righteously**
- **God can hate righteously**

Those things all belong to God alone. So the fact that God does something doesn't automatically make it all right for you and me to do it.

The Bible says that God Himself laid this stumblingstone.

- **It's a divider**
- **It's a test**
- **One person will trip over it**
- **Another person will rest upon it**

It is the work of God to set the sheep on the right hand and the goats on the left.
"...when the fullness of the time was come," the Bible says, *"God sent forth His Son,..."*[2]

Did you ever think about that? God sent Jesus into this world in probably the worst time for Him to be positively received.

- **The Jews were divided spiritually between the Sadducees and the Pharisees**
- **The Romans had occupied Israel and weren't too kind to the Jewish people as a whole**
- **Herod was on the throne and he was a jealous half Jew**

Why didn't God send Jesus while Moses was leading Israel, or better yet, while David was the King? He almost certainly would have been received better then.

Why didn't God send Jesus:
- **During the Reformation**
- **During one of the great periods of Revival we always hear about**
- **At the birth of religious liberty in the United States of America**

It's because God isn't interested in:
- **Quick**
- **Painless**
- **Shallow**

professions of faith in Christ.

He is looking for earnest sincere committed followers of the Lord.

B. A rock is not always offensive

Did you ever hear about the conversation between the ship's captain and the young signalman?

The captain was making headway in the dark when ahead he saw a light that right in his way. He had his signalman flash out in morse code that the vessel in front of him should change its course to avoid being hit. The light ahead of him flashed back that he would not change his position and that the ship should change course to avoid collision. The captain of the ship signaled back, "I am a Captain in the United States navy and I am in a battleship. I order you to move out of my way." The reply was, "I am the keeper of a lighthouse and I advise you to change your course."

In the dark of the night that lighthouse is either a blessing or a curse, depending upon whether the ship's captain believes his message.

The Bible says that Jesus Christ is either a stumbling stone or a cornerstone, depending on whether or not you believe His message.

THE BIBLE IS A STUMBLINGSTONE

1 Corinthians 1:23 (KJV)
But we preach Christ crucified, unto the Jews a stumblingblock, and unto the Greeks foolishness;

It's amazing how much controversy this book has created.

- **Thousands upon thousands have died just because they possessed this book**
- **Whole armies have been commissioned to hunt down and exterminate those that believed this book**
- **World religions have been established in opposition to this book**
- **World revivals have happened when people began to read this book**

One man, an unknown teacher, who lived in the early 1500's, tutoring a family's few children by day and translating the Bible from Greek into English by candlelight during the night. William Tyndale was executed at the age of 42, but the work he did touches your life still today. But at the very same time

Tyndale risked his life, and eventually gave his life for love of the Bible, there were others who absolutely hated it. Bishop Tunstall so hated the Bible that he gave huge sums of money to buy up and burn every Bible that Tyndale had printed. Tunstall didn't realize it, but rather than hurting the cause of the Word of God, he helped it. His purchase of Tyndale's first editions made Tyndale enough money to run a second, much higher quality edition.

As a preacher of the Word of God, I am often called upon to visit with those who are very sick or dying. It seems normal that, when I make that kind of visit, that I would pray and read some portion of the Bible. What I have discovered over the years is that:

- **Some people, in those life and death situations, find great comfort and blessing by the Bible**
- **Some people dislike even having the Bible read to them**

This book is a stumblinblock for many people.
In preparing for this chapter I found a website dedicated to pointing out God's cruelty.

The site begins with a quote from Robert Ingersoll, which reads,

> "According to "Samuel," David took a census of the people. This excited the wrath of Jehovah, and as a punishment he allowed David to choose seven years of famine, a flight of three months from pursuing enemies, or three days of pestilence. David, having confidence in God, chose the three days of pestilence; and thereupon, God, the compassionate, on account of the sin of David, killed seventy thousand innocent men. Under the same circumstances,

what would a devil have done? -- Robert Green
Ingersoll, "About the Holy Bible" (1894)"[2]

The Bible is a stumblingblock to the makers of that web site. And having said that, I make no apologies for
- **The Bible**
- **The God who gave us the Bible**
- **Believing the Bible**

For most people,

HEAVEN AND HELL IS A STUMBLINGSTONE

The largest religions in the world do not believe there is a heaven at all.

They have
- **Nirvana**
- **Reincarnation**
- **The creation of solar systems of our own**

The very concept of living eternally in a place that is God's and where God determines who does and doesn't go there is bothersome to them.

And then huge numbers of so called Bible believing Christians have questioned the existence of hell.
- **The Seventh Day Adventists**
- **The Jehovah's Witnesses**

Neither one believe in a literal burning hell. But frankly, neither does Billy Graham. Years and years ago Graham bought into the modernist arguments concerning the subject of hell and stopped preaching that hell was a place of literal fire.

The modern Bible scholars, producers of the NIV and other translations of the Bible that are opposed to the King James

Version, are quick to point out that in the Hebrew and the Greek, there is no such place as hell.
- **There is Tartarus**
- **There is Sheol**
- **There is Gehenna**

And they will claim that none of them describes a permanent place of literal fire and torments.

I just want to remind you that Jesus said,

Mark 9:43-48 (KJV)

And if thy hand offend thee, cut it off: it is better for thee to enter into life maimed, than having two hands to go into hell, into the fire that never shall be quenched:

Where their worm dieth not, and the fire is not quenched.

And if thy foot offend thee, cut it off: it is better for thee to enter halt into life, than having two feet to be cast into hell, into the fire that never shall be quenched:

Where their worm dieth not, and the fire is not quenched.

And if thine eye offend thee, pluck it out: it is better for thee to enter into the kingdom of God with one eye, than having two eyes to be cast into hell fire:

Where their worm dieth not, and the fire is not quenched.

Looks to me like Jesus believes hell is:
- **Literal**
- **Terrible**
- **Eternal**

The man who was my pastor when I surrendered to preach was named Roger Bellshaw. Pastor Belshaw was a construction worker – a welder from John Day, OR. One day he went out deer hunting with his wife's pastor, a Baptist preacher by the name of Richard Gosnell.

Pastor Belshaw said that they killed a deer and, as they began to clean and gut it, Pastor Gosnell asked him the question, "If you died today, do you know where you would go?"

To which Bro Belshaw answered, "I would go to hell." Brother Belshaw used to tell us, he didn't even question it. He understood that he was on his way to hell unless something changed. That's why he got saved. But to most people the very idea that God would create a place like hell is offensive to them.

Hell is a stumblingstone.

THE HOLINESS OF GOD IS A STUMBLINGSTONE

Isaiah 55:7-9 (KJV)

Let the wicked forsake his way, and the unrighteous man his thoughts: and let him return unto the LORD, and he will have mercy upon him; and to our God, for he will abundantly pardon.
For my thoughts are not your thoughts, neither are your ways my ways, saith the LORD.
For as the heavens are higher than the earth, so are my ways higher than your ways, and my thoughts than your thoughts.

An overriding principle of the Christian faith is that God is our standard. He gets to set the rules because He is our standard.

- **We do not question Him because He is our standard**
- **Reason and logic have a place in academics but not in faith because He is our standard**
- **Fair and unfair are irrelevant because God is our standard**

That principle really chaps most people. Everything in fallen and corrupted mankind screams that we are the standard. You listen to the way most Christians talk even and it sounds like they believe God exists for them.

- **He is obligated to make them wealthy**
- **He is obligated to give them health**
- **He is obligated to smooth away all of their troubles**
- **He is obligated to fix all the problems they created**

The largest congregations of some kind of Christendom have teachers telling them exactly how obligated God is to take care of them. And when it doesn't work out that way for them, they get very upset at God.

They stumble over God's holiness.

I just want to tell you:
- **When they trip over Jesus Christ – I will keep preaching Christ**
- **When they trip over the Word of God – I will keep taking them to the Bible**
- **When they trip over heaven and hell – I will keep warning them about hell**
- **When they trip over the holiness of God – I will still insist that God alone is our standard**

DON'T LET YOUR LIBERTY BE A STUMBLINGSTONE

1 Corinthians 8:9
But take heed lest by any means this liberty of your's become a stumblingblock to them that are weak.

I see three things to help me keep from tripping them over my liberty.

A. I am going to have to put some effort into it

That's what "take heed" means. If I want to obey this command of the Bible and not let my liberty be a stumblingblock, I am going to have to put some:
- **Thought**
- **Attention**
- **Energy**

behind it.

If I do the natural and easy thing, I will make them trip for sure.

Christian, how much effort do you put into being a help to people instead of a tripping hazard?

B. I am going to have to take heed in every area of my life
That's what "by any means" means.

I am going to have to learn to not take down my guard.
  - **At home**
  - **At work**
  - **At church**
  - **At the supermarket**
  - **At the filling station**
  - **When I am relaxing with friends**
  - **When I am stressing over a hurdle**
  - **When I am ministering to a class**

If I am going to avoid causing someone to trip over my liberty as a believer I am going to have to "take heed" at all times to be sure that at no time my liberty becomes a stumblingblock.

C. I am going to have to see myself as responsible
That's what "them that are weak" means.

I believe one of the most problematic things we have going on in American Christianity is a problem with how we view ourselves. Too many Christian view themselves as "the weak". They see themselves as the ones everyone else ought to be careful not to trip.

Too many Christians refuse to take responsibility for their own spiritual well being and for the good of others. They see themselves as the ones needing to be ministered to and not as the ones who ought to be ministering to others. They do not believe they are responsible if someone trips over them because they do not believe they are strong in the Lord.

My answer to that is "Get over it."

Conclusion
Someone is going to trip over Christ.
I can't help that.
Someone is going to trip over the Bible.
I can't do anything about that.
Someone is going to trip over heaven and hell
That's not a problem I can solve.
Someone is going to trip over the holiness of God
When it happens, it happens.

But no one need ever trip over your liberty or mine.
- **Take personal responsibility**

Step up to the plate
- **Accept that Christ hath strengthened you and ...**

...take heed lest by any means this liberty of yours become a stumblingblock to them that are weak.

[1] http://skepticsannotatedbible.com/cruelty/long.html. The site contains pages on topics such as:
- **Cruelty and violence in the Bible**
- **How many people has God killed?**
- **Bible atrocities**
- **Is anything cruel to a believer?**

[2] Galatians 4:4

Chapter Twenty-Five

HOW TO AVOID GETTING HUNG UP

Galatians 5:1 (KJV)

Stand fast therefore in the liberty wherewith Christ hath made us free, and be not entangled again with the yoke of bondage.

Galatia was a region, not a town; that's why Paul speaks here about the churches of Galatia.

- **It is not one universal church**
- **It is not even one regional church**

There were churches in the region of Galatia.

Apparently all of these churches were facing the same problem; a group of, what were then called Judaizers – we would call them "Messianic Jews," had infiltrated the area and began spreading a false gospel.

The entire letter should be considered Paul's attack on their false version of Christianity. I say it is an attack instead of a defense because the letter is very aggressive. Paul isn't even pretending to be nice. One writer called the epistle to the Galatians "Inspired Agitation."

When I read this a few things come to my mind. I picture an animal, fighting to get free of a trap.

A few years ago someone sent me a video of a horse that had somehow jumped through the window on the side of the horse trailer. The windows aren't very big and right now I can't remember the explanation of how it happened, but the horse was hanging half in and half out this window. If they don't do something, the horse is going to die there.

But the horse is afraid. A 2000 lbs animal is a very dangerous thing when it is afraid.

The video is maybe a half hour long of people trying different things to help this horse get free of its entanglement without the people getting hurt in the process. Good news is, the horse did survive and no one got hurt.

As I said, I do not remember the circumstances of why the horse tried to go through the window, but he would have been much safer if he had just been content to stay inside the trailer until they opened the door, wouldn't he?

Aren't we like that a lot?
- **We get ourselves in serious trouble because we try to fight our way out of the place God has us.**
- **We get ourselves into more trouble when we try to fight His will when He tells us how to get out of the trouble we are in.**

When I read the word "entangled" this week, my mind pictured a bull rider getting "hung up" in his rope. In my much younger years, when I rode bulls, there was a bull rider I knew by the name of Bruce Kimsey. He and his brother Turman, were from Finley and were usually at all the same rodeos I was at. I would not say we were friends, but we knew each other very well. In my office I have a picture of me riding a bull, Turman is in the background of that picture.

Anyway, this story is about Bruce. Bruce had a nasty habit of getting hung up in his rope A LOT. Bruce got so psyched up about riding that he would forget to let go, even when he got bucked off or his eight seconds was up. If you don't let go you just get thrown around on the side of that bull! It's a dangerous place to be. Fortunately there are guys there to help a bull rider out when he is hung up. Whenever Bruce would forget to let go, one of the bull fighters would start hollering, "Let go Bruce, Let Go!" but after a half second one of those bull fighters would jump on the side of the bull between Bruce and the bull's head, to protect him, and the other would jump on the other side of the bull to try to get his hand unentangled.

My wife and I don't have any TV stations at home, but we do have internet so I get to watch bull riding highlights just about every day.

- **Friday is "Flint Friday where they show the stupid jokes of Flint Rasmussen, the Professional Bull Rider's official rodeo clown.**
- **Thursday is "Throw back Thursday", where they show a bull ride from a few years ago.**
- **Monday they show a winning ride.**
- **Tuesday they show a top bull who bucked off his rider really fast.**
- **Wednesday is "Wreck Wednesday" where they show a bull rider getting stomped on by a bull.**

A couple of weeks ago Flint Rasmussen did a spoof on the difference between athletes. He said, "Have you ever watched a soccer game? These professional soccer players get kicked in the shin and they flop around on the ground and scream until someone comes and carries them off the field." A bull rider will:

- **Take a head butt with the horns of a bull**
- **Get stepped on by 2 and a half tons of bull**
- **Get thrown up against the fence**

Then he will stand up, wave his hat to the crowd and walk out of the arena on his own two feet. Some of the most amazing videos on "Wreck Wednesday" are those of the bull fighters helping a guy who is hung up, entangled in his rope.

My message this morning will be a simile.

I want to use the bull rider to illustrate the meaning of Galatians 5:1 (KJV)
Stand fast therefore in the liberty wherewith Christ hath made us free, and be not entangled again with the yoke of bondage.

A simile likens one thing to another thing. You can always tell when someone is using a simile because it will always say, "This is like that."

In our simile today
- **The bull is like the world (worldliness)**
- **The bull rider is like the Christian**
- **The bull fighter is like our Saviour**

THE BULL

Galatians 5:1 (KJV)
Stand fast therefore in the liberty wherewith Christ hath made us free, and be not entangled again with the yoke of bondage.

I have a question. What would ever possess a person to strap himself on the back of a 2000 lbs bull? You'll hear the rodeo announcer describe him sometimes as "2000 lbs of 'mean'".

I have been asked that question and for me, honestly, I didn't have much of a choice. My family was a rodeo family. My grandfather was the president of an amateur rodeo club in Finley, WA. As far back as I can remember we rode grandpa's steers and cows out in his pasture. Grandpa would put a rope around the cow's neck, a bull rope around the cow's rib cage, set one of us kids on it and turn 'er loose. Would get bucked off into the prickly pear cactus and grandma would snip off the needles at the skin tape which was a slice of potato or apple over them and tell us to get tough.

All of this was when I was five or six years old. I know that because I was afraid to ride calves in the rodeo, and so thinking this was a good idea, I promised him when I was eight, I would enter calf riding in the rodeo. Grandpa was the president of the rodeo club. June 8, 1966, my eighth birthday – my present from Grandpa Tiwater was a rodeo so I could enter my first calf riding event. For me it just wasn't an option.

Now I said the bull is like the world. In real life – have you ever had an option whether you are going to ride this world or not?
- **You came into this world crying**
- **You might have come into this world scared**
- **You came into this world perfectly happy with where you were before you came into this world**

but you came into this world nonetheless!

Growing up
- **I rode calves until I reached a certain age**
- **I rode steers until I reached a certain age**
- **I rode cows until I reached a certain age**

Frankly, I wasn't planning on riding bulls. My dad was a team roper, and I was pretty good with horses. I wanted to be a team roper. But then came the day when dad sold his horses. Grandpa Tiwater had died and just about the same time, my family quit rodeoing and moved up into the Blue Mountains. I could not afford to have my own team roping horse, but rodeo was in my blood. Bull riding was the only thing I could afford to do.

Is it not true that a lot of the time we do what we do in the world, not because we like it, but because we don't know what else to do?

The Christian is like

THE BULL RIDER

Galatians 5:1 (KJV)
Stand fast therefore in the liberty wherewith Christ hath made us free, and be not entangled again with the yoke of bondage.

The Christian's life is entirely different. He is in this world, but he is not of this world.
- **He strives for mastery over the world in him**
- **He longs to use his life for the glory of the Lord**

Romans 12:2 (KJV)
And be not conformed to this world: but be ye transformed by the renewing of your mind, that ye may prove what is that good, and acceptable, and perfect, will of God.

The bull rider faces up to his adversary. He ties himself onto the back of that powerful animal knowing full well that he can't ever control it, but he does not have to let it control him either. He hopes to stay there eight seconds. When the buzzer sounds, he is free.

That's life. We are only here a short time. As a believer in the Lord Jesus Christ I may not be able to change the course of the world, but I do not have to let it change me. I can head into my life full throttle for Jesus Christ. I can live my life for His glory and honor.

I only have to do it for a little bit and then contest is over. I am free – heaven bound!

Once in a while though, the cowboy gets hung up – entangled again in the rope. He is finished with the bull, but the bull isn't finished with him. I have known a good number of Christians get hung up in this world.

- **It might be a sinful habit**
- **It might be a worldly love**
- **It might be a religious background**

It's got ahold of him. He is entangled in it. It is at this stage that steps in,

THE BULL FIGHTERS

Galatians 5:1 (KJV)
Stand fast therefore in the liberty wherewith Christ hath made us free, and be not entangled again with the yoke of bondage.

These guys are incredible athletes. They work, nowadays, in a trinity – three guys, each one with specific jobs. They all look a lot alike. In action, you would have a difficult time telling them apart but they all know what their jobs to do – their function in the arena. Their job is to risk life and limb to make the rider free.

The Christian has a Trinity on his side too:

- **God the Father, who makes all things work together for good**
- **God the Son, who went to the cross and died in our place**
- **God the Holy Spirit, who regenerates us when we ask for salvation and seals (protects) us until the day of redemption**

Have you ever gotten confused which one of the three you are praying too? Sometimes it's hard for us to know which one to call on! Never fear, they know exactly what their role is in your life and mine.

Conclusion

You know why a Christian gets caught back up in worldliness? It's because he forgets who it is he is trusting. When he got saved he said he was done with the world, but the world wasn't done with him.

It can be a sinful entanglement.

He stops trusting the Holy Spirit to give him power to obey God instead of sin.

It can be a rich entanglement.

He stops laying up treasures in heaven instead of on earth.

It could be, as was the case in these churches in Galatia, a religious entanglement.

He stops seeing Christ as the absolute Saviour and wants to add some of his own good works into his salvation.

Galatians 5:1 (KJV)

Stand fast therefore in the liberty wherewith Christ hath made us free, and be not entangled again with the yoke of bondage.

Fight for your freedom! But don't do it like a wild animal who could hurt the ones who want to help you. Fight for your freedom by trusting God:

- **He has saved you in the Person of Christ**
- **He has sealed you in the Person of the Holy Ghost**
- **He has promised that all things will work together for good in the Person of the Father**

Chapter Twenty-Six

LIBERTY AND LOVE

Galatians 5:13 (KJV)

For, brethren, ye have been called unto liberty; only use not liberty for an occasion to the flesh, but by love serve one another.

One of the realizations that the founders of our country came to during the process of organizing a new form of government was that they were in a unique position to advance, not only their own purposes, but also those of the whole nation.

It probably began with Thomas Jefferson's Declaration of Independence which, when read around the colonies, was applied all sorts of ways that Jefferson and the others founders probably hadn't initially intended:

- **Women rights**
- **Slave's rights**
- **The ability for the average person to possess land**
- **Voting rights**

What happened was that this new freedom gave the people of the United States of America an opportunity to serve one another.

Galatians 5:13 tells us that we have a choice how we will use the liberty we have as Christians:

- **We can use it "...*for an occasion to the flesh*"**

I am saved and nobody can take that away from me so I will do as I please.

- **We can use it to "...*by love serve one another*"**

I want to focus your thoughts today on that phrase, "...*by love serve...*"

There is a connection between love and service that runs all the way through the New Testament.

A. Love is a motivator of service …
John 14:15 (KJV)
If ye love me, keep my commandments.

Keeping Christ's commandments would, of course, be a form of serving Him.

Love motivates service. There are things, for instance, that I would do for Anita and my boys that would not feel anywhere near as motivated to do for anyone else. The reason is simple, I love them. It's not that I don't love other people, but I love them more.

As I think about it, the more I love a person, the more compelled I am to cheerfully do things for them.

Love is a motivator for service.

B. Love is a "metamorphoser" of service …
1 John 5:3 (KJV)
For this is the love of God, that we keep his commandments: and his commandments are not grievous.

Love changes the nature and character of service.
1. Some service is out of necessity
A person needs a paycheck so they take a job.
- **They would probably prefer to stay at home**
- **They may have other goals they want to accomplish**
- **They might have children they miss while they are at work**
but they serve because they need to.

2. Some service is out of constraint

I guess a little bit of schadenfruede in me that drives me to like this story so much:
Amazing Grace, no doubt one of the favorite hymns in this church, was written by John Newton. Newton was a much-loved minister in England in the 1800's, but as a young man he was pretty much a loser. Newton had fallen in love with, a girl several years younger than he was and, especially because of her age, he was not allowed to see her. One day he was walking through the streets, probably in a daze daydreaming about Mary. He was caught by a group of sailors and pressed into service for the Royal Navy. Apparently in those days, if a British Naval ship needed more sailors, the captain came to port and sent his sailors out hunting. If they found an able bodied man by himself, they caught him, forced him onboard and made them serve in the navy. Serving in the navy wasn't something Newton wanted to do. It was something he was made to do.

- **I know people who took a job because they needed to make money and learned to love their job**
- **I know some who didn't want to be in the military but learned to love their time in the service**

Love has the ability to change service to something that is not grievous.

Genesis 29:20 (KJV)
And Jacob served seven years for Rachel; and they seemed unto him but a few days, for the love he had to her.

C. Love is a producer of service
This is where I want to take the remainder of this message. Galatians 5:13 says, "*...by love serve...*"

The Bible tells us to embrace the liberty we have as Christians, love it; and then let service to others flow out of that love.

LOVING SERVICE ENDURES DIFFERENCES

1 Corinthians 13:4-8 (KJV)

Charity suffereth long, and is kind; charity envieth not; charity vaunteth not itself, is not puffed up,
Doth not behave itself unseemly, seeketh not her own, is not easily provoked, thinketh no evil;
Rejoiceth not in iniquity, but rejoiceth in the truth;
Beareth all things, believeth all things, hopeth all things, endureth all things.
Charity never faileth: but whether there be prophecies, they shall fail; whether there be tongues, they shall cease; whether there be knowledge, it shall vanish away.

These verses are most often used to try to describe the relationship between a man and his wife. I suppose that's all right, but it is not the primary application. Charity, as it is found in the Bible, is a peculiar type of love that describes the Christian's relationship with his or her church. "Loving service" is just about as good a definition of charity as you will find.

What I want you to notice right now is how much of this charity is about putting aside differences:

- **Charity suffereth long**
- **Is not easily provoked**
- **Thinketh no evil**
- **Beareth all things**
- **Endureth all things**
- **Charity never faileth**

As a Christian you are free to spiritually "do as you please."

- **You can tell a member of the church off if you want**
- **You can talk badly about them behind their back if you want**

- **You can personally shun a member of the church if you want**
- **You can quit the church and go find a brand new bunch of people to tell off, talk about behind their back and shun if you want**

Galatians 5:13 teaches you to do something completely different than that. Galatians 5:13 teach us:
- **To hang in there with one another**
- **To put aside differences**
- **To embrace as a friend**
- **To refrain from saying those mean things**
- **To stay committed to the same church**

Loving service endures differences.

LOVING SERVICE EMBRACES OTHERS AS FAMILY

Hebrews 13:1 (KJV)
Let brotherly love continue.

Right away I notice that this theme of enduring is associated with this passage too. I want to focus on a new thought and that this love is "brotherly love." It is family love. Loving service welcomes new souls into your family.

I think maybe the most dramatic illustration of this is the story of Jesus on the cross.
John 19:27 (KJV)
Then saith he to the disciple, Behold thy mother! And from that hour that disciple took her unto his own home.

John assumed the responsibility to care for Jesus' mother Mary, and Mary accepted it. The same concept can be found in:
- **Isaac and Rebecca, who agreed to marry having not even known each other**

- **Boaz and Ruth, Ruth wasn't even a Jew, but was invited into the family of Jesus Christ**
- **David and Abigail, she was another man's wife, but when Nabal died, David welcomed her**

On a different level but something very similar is Paul's love for Timothy whom he calls his son in the faith.

Loving service embraces others into our family.
- **We are closer than partners**
- **We are much more than contacts**
- **We are more than business associates**
- **We are not just peers or companions**

- **We are joint heirs with Jesus Christ**
- **We are each sons of God**

We have each been born of the Spirit and washed in the blood of Jesus Christ.

Loving service embraces one another into our family.

LOVING SERVICE SACRIFICES FOR OTHERS

Romans 12:10 (KJV)
Be kindly affectioned one to another with brotherly love; in honour preferring one another;

All of us who have been Christians for very long know that the true love is giving expecting nothing in return. It is what God did for us when He gave His only begotten Son.
- **He gave while we were yet sinners**
- **He gave even if we reject Christ as the Saviour for our sin**
- **He gave because He first loved us**

Loving service gives sacrificially.

Loving service gives:
- **No questions asked**

- **No expectations raised**
- **No follow-up necessary**

It's wonderful when it happens that our love is reciprocated. If it has to be reciprocated, however, it isn't really even wonderful, its just return on investment.

Conclusion
When you trusted Jesus as your Saviour, you were set free.
- **Free from the guilt of sin**
- **Free from the bondage of religion**
- **Free from the fear of eternal hell**

Jesus freely gave that liberty to you. He will never take it away. Galatians 5:13 asks you to choose how you will use that liberty.
- **Will you use it for selfish, fleshly purposes?**
- **Will you, by love serve one another?**

Made in the USA
Monee, IL
09 July 2026

56747434R00142